HITCHHIKING
FROM VIETNAM

HITCHHIKING FROM VIETNAM:
SEEKING THE OX

A MEMOIR
BY
RICHARD CHAMBERLIN

SPINOZA PUBLISHING
MADISON, WISCONSIN

Author's Note: Some of the names and identifying characteristics of the persons included in this book have been changed.

Published in the United States of America
by Spinoza Publishing
Post Office Box 14768
Madison, WI 53708

www.spinozapublishing.com

ISBN: 978-0-9789093-0-7

First Edition

An earlier version of Chapter 14: Dexter's Drones, appeared in the publication *Mobius: The Journal of Social Change*.

Book design and composition by Julie Murkette
Cover photo © Bart Sadowski

Desolate through forests and fearful jungles,
He is seeking an Ox which he does not find
Up and down dark, nameless, wide-flowing rivers,
In deep mountain thickets he treads many bypaths.
Bone-tired, heart weary, he carries on his search
For this is something which he cannot find.
At evening he hears cicadas chirping in the trees.

Kikuan Shien – A Chinese Zen Master of the twelfth century
— from *The Way of Zen* by Alan Watts

Acknowledgments

Many people have read drafts of this book over the years and made helpful suggestions. Fellow writer Richard Ely, who I met while we were driving cab at Union, gave generously of his time, and critiqued the entire manuscript. I'd also like to thank Bill Wheeler and Kate Schachter for their helpful suggestions. The members of my writing group, formed after a meeting at the 2004 Wisconsin Book Festival, were invaluable in helping me shave off the rough edges and add greater depth to my chapters. They are: Marylu Green, Kirsten Houtman, Karen Milstein and Jason Stein. Friends and family have helped including my wife, Judi, who has been a constant source of moral support; my mother Marjory, who believed in me as a writer when I didn't even believe in myself, and who passed away recently; and my sisters Bette Chamberlin and Sandra Chamberlin Michaels of Montclair, New Jersey. I'd also like to thank my friends who have trusted me enough to let me use their real names; you know who you are. Last, I'd like to thank my designer/typesetter, Julie Murkette, for her great cover design and magically taking a raw manuscript and turning it into a book.

I DEDICATE THIS BOOK TO MY MOTHER, MARJORY.

CONTENTS

PART FOUR - THE TRIP BACK

PREFACE

THE MORE THINGS CHANGE the more they stay the same.

In early August of 1964 President Johnson, with the help of a compliant press, convinced Americans that North Vietnamese patrol boats attacked a US destroyer innocently operating in international waters. In response, Congress passed the Gulf of Tonkin Resolution, which gave Johnson broad powers to expand the war. Ten years later, over 58,000 American soldiers had been killed and a generation of young adults had become disenchanted with their leaders.

Flash forward to October 11, 2002. On that day, President George W. Bush convinced Congress to give him the authorization to wage a preemptive war against Iraq, fearing it would use "weapons of mass destruction" to attack the United States. In March of 2003 we invaded Iraq and deposed its dictator, Saddam Hussein. When no weapons of mass destruction were found, Bush switched his rationale for the invasion to establishing a beachhead of freedom and democracy in the Middle East. As I write this, Iraq is locked into a civil war resulting in a slaughter of immense proportions. We are decimating our army and there is no end in sight.

Both of these wars were sold to the American people using manipulated intelligence reports. In both wars soldiers have come home disillusioned and suffering in large numbers from Post Traumatic Stress Disorder, unable to reintegrate into society. Whether it was in My Lai or Haditha, the frustrations of fighting an insurgency have led to the massacre of civilians.

Every war veteran will wrestle with the demons of their own personal war and its meaning. They will ask themselves if it was worth the sacrifice. Their quest for meaning will affect their attitude toward their country, their family, their culture and themselves for as long as they live.

In this book I have tried to give the reader a window into my mind as I struggled to make sense of a society that was being consumed by its own contradictions just as America is today.

The book begins in 1975 in Madison, Wisconsin, liberal home of the University of Wisconsin and mid-west epicenter of violent anti-war protests during the late 1960's. President Richard Nixon had resigned in disgrace a year earlier and the former Vice President Gerald Ford was now president. The North Vietnamese had taken Saigon. A TV show called *All in the Family*, featuring a bigot and his hippie son-in-law, premiered on CBS. Muhammad Ali defeated Joe Frazier in the "Thrilla' in Manila," and William Henry Gates III dropped out of Harvard. Two years later he started a small computer company called Microsoft. The U.S. economy was in a recession, gasoline had jumped to fifty-seven cents a gallon nationwide, and the Dow Jones hit a high of 880.

The American psyche was in a state of meltdown. People had lost faith in government due to a general feeling of malaise after ten bloody years of the war in Vietnam and many turned to religion. Evangelists like Pat Robertson, Billy Graham, Jerry Falwell, Jim Baker and Hal Lindsay were shaking the foundations of established churches with what was called a Third Great

Awakening of religious fervor in America. A generation that had grown up during the turbulent 60's began to look inward for personal growth. For those who rejected Judeo-Christian traditions, Eastern faiths such as Buddhism and Hinduism became popular, and gurus attracted large numbers of followers. Still others used mind-altering drugs as a shortcut to gaining higher levels of spiritual understanding. It was a confusing time filled with hope and despair, faith and skepticism, confidence and doubt, but most of all it was a period of great change. Those changes continue to effect how we live our lives in the twenty-first century.

This is the story of a hitchhiking trip I took back then and some things I learned.

Richard Chamberlin
March 2007

PART ONE

MADISON

1
THE LAUNDRY
Madison – Spring 1975

I REALLY WASN'T LOOKING for spiritual enlightenment. I just wanted to get inside to do my laundry. A cold damp wind lashed across my face, typical early spring weather for Madison, Wisconsin. As I walked quickly down Williamson Street lugging two pillowcases full of dirty clothes, the chipped, faded paint and torn asphalt shingles of the small wood frame houses along the sidewalk bore testimony to the severity of the seasons. Swollen buds on twigs stood stiff and naked like reluctant young recruits anxiously awaiting the first warm breezes of spring. The receding snows had left behind months of windblown garbage and piles of dog excrement in shallow puddles on the sidewalk. I longed for warmth and greenery after a long, brutal Midwestern winter.

When I got to the run-down laundromat it was deserted. I threw my clothes into the washer, dumped in some soap, slid two quarters into the tarnished silver slots and slammed them home. The machine began to hum and fill with water. I sat down on a tipsy three-legged plastic chair and tried to keep my balance while reading a stray newspaper, a reminder that a human world existed beyond the dank stillness of a room populated with aging machines. Suddenly the washer began to thud dangerously like a drunken Sumo wrestler.

I got up and rearranged the load. As I walked back to my chair, the door creaked open and a long-haired fellow entered carrying two large black garbage bags full of laundry. He wore a plain white tunic, white pants and sandals, and glanced toward me with large, dark, almond-shaped eyes.

While only a glance, it stunned me. I turned away. What was it about his eyes? They seemed to look right through me. The stranger had a large scar on the left side of his face and part of an ear was missing. He placed his bags on a folding table, brushed back his dark hair, and took some coins from a woven satchel that hung from his neck. He walked over to the soap dispenser and bought three boxes of detergent, limping with a slightly exaggerated side-to-side motion like Charlie Chaplin. I pretended to read the newspaper.

He went back to the folding table, picked up each of the black bags and wrestled their contents into the washers. He added the soap, put the coins in the slots, then hobbled back to a chair on the other side of the room where he sat down and began reading from a small black book. When my washer clicked off, I transferred my clothes to a dryer and snuck another glance at him. He looked out of place, like a mystic from another dimension who had re-materialized on the steps of the laundromat. I wanted to find out more about him but couldn't think of anything to say. After my dryer stopped I took my clothes out and began folding them. When the stranger's washer shut off he gathered his clothes in his arms, threw them into a couple nearby dryers, dug around in his satchel and came up with a dollar bill.

He walked over to where I was folding my clothes and said, "Excuse me. Do you have change for a dollar?"

"I don't know; I'll see," I said, digging into my pockets. I had two quarters and some change. I gave him what I had.

"Thanks a lot," he said smiling. "My name is Ken-Adi."

I wasn't sure I should extend my hand because it was so conventional but did it anyway. "I'm Richard," I said. He reached out in a similar manner and we shook. His hands were thick, yet his grip was surprisingly warm and gentle.

The cosmic eyes softened a little. He went back to the dryer and I resumed folding my clothes. By the time I was done, his dryer had stopped. He emptied the contents on a table and began folding.

"Hey, Richard, could you help me fold something?" he called out as I loaded up my laundry bag.

I went over to his table, and he handed me the end of a long gauzy piece of cloth.

"What's this for?" I asked.

"That's for my turban. Fold it in half lengthwise and then just hold it."

I did as he said, and he began folding it slowly, reverently into wedges, the way someone folds a flag.

"Do you belong to an ashram around here?" I finally asked.

"I live in the one over there on Johnson Street," he replied, as if everyone knew where it was. When I hesitated, he added, "The Tri-Unity Center. Yogi Bajan is my spiritual master and I'm studying massage."

I didn't know Yogi Bajan from Yogi Bear so merely nodded my head, hoping that my silence would be mistaken for understanding.

When we were done, he thanked me and invited me to stop by the ashram sometime. I never did because I had no intention of joining a religious cult. I had never been a member of a church and wasn't about to take up wearing a turban. Most of the time I wasn't even sure if there was a God. If there was, I didn't think he exerted much control over people's lives. Yet I had an intuition that there was some sort of spiritual force in the universe, a force that I wanted to connect with. I had been looking for a philosophy to live by ever since I had returned from Vietnam in '69, yet was still reluctant to let anyone else tell me what to think. I wanted to figure things out myself.

During the mid-seventies, with the Vietnam War over, the generation that had brought about massive street demonstrations and changes in the social order began to turn inward. Pop psychologists and spiritual leaders emerged to take advantage of the new market for self-fulfillment. While I never intended to immerse myself in any of the spiritual movements, curiosity drove me to nibble around the edges, so I nibbled at the idea that Ken-Adi could be my guru.

A couple of years earlier a friend of mine named Dave Crum, who I'd met while working as a newspaper reporter in Indiana, got me interested in a former Harvard University professor-turned-guru named Baba Ram Dass. Dave loaned me his book, *Be Here Now*. The book seemed to say, don't try so hard. There are forces at work on you that you have no knowledge of. Accept life and let enlightenment come to you when the time is right. This advice was something I felt comfortable with during a period of my life when I wasn't sure where I was going. Although the concept was simple, I would soon find out that applying it was more difficult than I had imagined.

2
ZUMBACH'S SUIT
Madison – Spring 1975

WHEN SPRING FINALLY CAME to Madison, magnolias burst from their pods to reveal dazzling white and pink swatches of color amidst the brown and gray sticks of winter. Maple leaves unfurled, exposing their delicate green food factories to the sun. Outside restaurants the smells of pizza and freshly baked bread tempted strollers.

In early May most of Madison's alternative community turned out to see Ram Dass at the University of Wisconsin. He was giving a talk at the Student Union South. Dave and I were going to see him once in Indiana, but I couldn't get away from work. I was determined not to miss him again.

However, I wasn't sure what to wear because my lifestyle had been in a state of flux. My white gauzy, embroidered hippie tunic clashed with my short hair. "Damn it," I thought. "Why did I have to get my hair cut so soon?" After trying on a couple outfits, I decided that since a guru couldn't be fooled, I'd go as myself and wore corduroy pants, a western-style shirt with snaps and cowboy boots.

When I entered the meeting room an oppressively sweet odor of strawberry incense filled the air. The bald Krishnas were there in orange, flowing robes. Several had a long shock of hair growing from their otherwise bald heads. A band of Sikhs with white turbans and others sat on the floor. However, most of the people dressed more conventionally, so I began to relax. I didn't look as out-of-place as I had feared.

A muffled, almost imperceptible hum began to build like the murmuring of tires on a freeway in the early morning. When someone began to twang away on a sitar the humming gently took on vowels and became "Ommmm, Ommm, Ommmm . . ." The room vibrated with a heightened anticipation. Everyone was waiting. Waiting for Ram Dass. Older people took the few chairs next to the wall, so I sat on the floor and crossed my legs. Soon the heels of my boots bit into my thighs. Sandals would have been a better choice. I removed the boots, but now my tailbone chafed against the hard terrazzo floor.

Next to me was a long-haired young man sitting in a full-lotus position, his toes showing through the bends in his knees. Who was I trying to kid? I didn't belong here. My position wasn't even a half-lotus and I was still uncomfortable.

The sitar whined lackadaisically and the incense got thicker. Through the smoky mist, I saw a man with long, wiry, grayish hair and a mid-length beard leaning against a wall. He wore a short sleeved shirt and slacks. It was Ram Dass, a spectator at his own lecture.

Soon he began to make his way toward the microphone, casually stepping between the bodies and doing a little swoop and sway dance as he walked, smiling radiantly at each person he passed.

When he reached the microphone, he rolled his eyes toward heaven and continued to sway until the sounds of the sitar and tamburas faded into silence.

He slowly lowered his gaze and looked around the room.

"Has anyone ever heard the story of Zumbach's suit?" he asked.

Silence.

"Well, I'm determined to tell it until everybody has," he said smiling.

"Once upon a time there was a tailor named Zumbach known far and wide for his skill," Ram Dass began. "One day a man came to him and asked to have a suit made. The tailor worked swiftly and in a short time had assembled a fine looking suit. But when the man tried it on, one sleeve was too long.

'No problem,' said Zumbach. 'Just drop your shoulder a bit.'" Ram Dass dropped his shoulder.

"But there was another problem. The other sleeve was too short. Again Zumbach saw no reason for alarm and showed the man how to draw up his arm when he walked." Ram Dass raised his other shoulder.

"At long last, after adjusting a few more defects, the man reluctantly paid for the suit. He was walking down the street when a stranger stopped him and asked if his suit was made by Zumbach, the tailor.

'Why yes,' replied the man. 'How could you tell?'

'Because,' replied the stranger, 'only a tailor as skilled as Zumbach could fit a misshapen person like you.'"

Everyone laughed.

"Many people find a spiritual movement and try to fit themselves into it," he went on. "The Hare Krishnas are always happy, happy, happy." Ram Dass jumped up and down, smiled and twinkled his fingers in the air. Even the Hare Krishnas laughed.

Ram Dass stopped smiling and his face went blank. "The Zen Buddhists are always stern and serious," he said in a monotone, holding the pose for a few seconds before smiling.

"Don't get caught in the spiritual trap," he said. "Find the practice that's most comfortable to you. Don't worry. If you are listening to your heart you will know when to hold back and when to move forward."

This is what I had been waiting to hear. At last there was someone who understood my spiritual longing. At last I had connected with someone who wasn't out to rip me off and try to make me accept a belief system I wasn't comfortable with. I immediately felt a spiritual closeness with Ram Dass, a closeness I wish I'd had with my own father, a salesman who had never quite closed the deal with his son.

Toward the end of his talk, Ram Dass led a meditation, and asked us to sit quietly and breathe in and out.

"Imagine that you are breathing out all the stale, black air you have been accumulating in your lungs and you are breathing in fresh, clean air," he said.

Slowly I sucked air into my lungs, then expelled it.

Next he said, "Imagine there is a little being of pure light that looks exactly like you, sitting in the middle of your body where the pit of your stomach is."

As my eyes closed, I gave Ram Dass total control of my thoughts.

"Now imagine that this being grows to the size of your body. Your head contains his head. His arms are in your arms. You and he are one." Ram Dass intoned each phrase slowly and evenly so that everybody would have time to get in touch with their spirit and be ready for the next phase.

"Now he grows again and encompasses all the people in this room. He is pure light. Breathe in and out slowly and deeply."

My mind became still, aware only of my breath.

"He becomes even larger and covers the entire city of Madison. The Capitol is inside his belly. Breathe slow and deep. You and he are the same."

I began to feel my body become lighter.

"He expands . . . again . . . and his hands . . . touch together . . . as he embraces . . ." (long pause) ". . . the earth."

My eyes closed and I became aware of little points of light twinkling in the blackness of my consciousness.

"Slowly . . . he grows again . . . and his hands touch the outermost planets of the solar system. The sun . . . is in . . . your heart. Breathe slow and quiet."

I felt my spirit reaching out into the vast nothingness of space and filling it with a warm, loving glow.

"And now . . . your molecules are racing outward at the speed of light . . . into the limitless universe . . . you have no body. You . . . and the universe . . . are one."

For an indeterminate amount of time, Ram Dass left us out there, floating around in space. Then, gently, he began to bring everyone back to this solar system, this earth, this city, this building, and finally, to this body.

Sitars began to twang and lazy, thick, trails of incense spiraled slowly into the air. A radiantly smiling Ram Dass, his eyes half closed and his pupils rolled up, began a slow shuffle toward the door. People came forward to hug him, tears of gratitude running down their faces. A young man with a scruffy beard came up to him and Ram Dass rapped him in the forehead. The young man fell back with a stunned expression on his face. I was next. I stood waiting for a spark of recognition to bridge the distance between us. He came closer. I just wanted our eyes to meet if only for a second, just a moment of connection.

But Ram Dass kept walking past me as if I weren't even there, the totally blissful expression still on his face. He wandered out the door, surrounded by adoring followers, and vanished.

Disappointment washed over me. We were soul mates with so much in common. The academic establishment rejected us both. We had both taken LSD. We were both searching for another way to live in this world. Why didn't he notice me?

A couple days later I planted myself in front of the painted golden Buddha in my living room and tried Ram Dass' meditation on a foam rubber pad. I imagined exhaling all the stale, bad air and inhaling all the fresh, good air. I expanded my body to encompass the whole universe then brought it back to earth. Soon I began to feel more relaxed and less critical of myself. When I read from *Be Here Now*, it was easier to identify with my spirit, but my ego told me that I should get back into journalism. My spirit answered back that I was already enough. I liked the message I got from my spirit, yet that pesky ego kept whispering in my ear, "You have failed." I knew that the tug-of-war between these two paradigms would have to be resolved before I could get my life back on track.

3
THE PEOPLE'S REPUBLIC OF MADISON
Spring 1974

I WAS BORN IN Madison and spent the first four years of my life there. Our family lived in a modest two-story frame house on Moland Street near the Oscar Meyer's meat packing plant.

My earliest memory is when the back yard flooded after a heavy rain and I floated away in my sandbox. I don't know how it was buoyant enough to float, or why the yard flooded, but when I used a stick to reach for a leaf, I fell overboard and had to be rescued by my mother. This was my first realization that life could be dangerous.

I remembered being in a neighborhood parade, the kind where kids were supposed to dress up in goofy costumes and ride their bicycles down the street. It was a big deal for the parents who walked alongside the kids and took pictures. My dad saved a snapshot of me on a tiny tricycle dressed like a clown in baggy coveralls with a big red lipstick border painted around my mouth. I felt self-conscious being the only kid in the parade with an elaborate costume.

When my sister Bette was born I passed out candy and cigars to the workers in the airplane hanger at Wisconsin Central Airlines where my father now worked as a salesman.

My mother, who met my father while working as a piano player for a dancing school where he taught tap, was now busy raising her family.

We could have lived the all-American life with our future prosperity assured if we had remained in Madison. Instead, looking for adventure and a break from the brutal winters, we moved to Miami, only to encounter a transient tourist economy and hustler mentality where it was hard to support a growing family. I left Miami when I graduated from junior college and migrated north, ending up in Chicago after four years in the Navy, including two deployments to Viet Nam. Returning to Madison after an absence of twenty-six years was my attempt to recapture a lost sense of stability. However, I was in for a big surprise. Madison had changed and the tumult of the Sixties left a contagion of rebellion that rocked the city to its core.

As I drove into town from Chicago in the spring of 1974, I was excited to be starting over in a beautiful new town. From Interstate 90-94 I saw the State Capitol, its white dome jutting up prominently on top of a hill between two lakes, Monona and Mendota. I had heard those lakes held huge game fish, like northerns and muskies, as well as the smaller perch and crappies. I made a note to myself to buy a fishing rod and try my luck. Beyond the Capitol the city spread out in all directions.

I exited the Interstate, headed west on Broadway, then turned north on Monona Drive, a commercial strip which gradually became the more residential Atwood Avenue. Here, the sturdy houses lining the road and built by German immigrants, were neat and clean with freshly mowed lawns.

I crossed the Yahara River, a canal that connected the two lakes. The houses had smaller yards and were closer together, giving the neighborhood a cozy look. I drove past St. Vincent's thrift shop, the Crystal Corner Bar, Dolly's home-cooking restaurant and a small print shop. The neighborhood, located near former factories, reflected the working class nature of the East Side. It was settled at the turn of the century and once was a center of industrial production. As the country shifted more toward a service economy, the factories closed and were converted to small shops and warehouses.

Williamson Street turned into King, which ran uphill toward the Capitol Square. At the top was a large, glass-walled bank that reflected the image of the massive white marble Capitol dome. The lawn around the Capitol was shaded with large oaks and maples and across the street were professional office buildings and retail stores.

West of the Capitol, Mifflin Street descended into a student neighborhood near the University of Wisconsin. I parked near the Mifflin Street Grocery Co-op, bought some peaches, then sat under a maple tree and ate my fruit. Unlike Williamson Street, Mifflin Street was a student ghetto and became a hub of anti-war sentiment during the Vietnam conflict. Daily demonstrations grew confrontational as students attempted to shut down the University through boycotts and sit-ins.

The unrest spread to the student ghettos. In the spring of 1969, the city refused to grant a permit for a "block party" on West Mifflin Street. The lack of a permit only exacerbated resentment and the residents became determined to take back their street by blocking traffic and holding their own party. After police tried unsuccessfully to clear the street, fights erupted, cops started firing cans of tear gas and people were dragged from their houses. The National Guard tried to control the spreading foment and soldiers with bayonets, jeeps and armored personnel carriers patrolled the campus.

A year later, on August 24, 1970, a small band of radicals bombed Sterling Hall because it housed the Math Army Research

Center where work was being conducted in support of the war. The bomb was a van loaded with two thousand pounds of ammonium nitrate. One of the bombers called the police to clear the building, but the bomb went off prematurely and a researcher was killed. The anti-war movement lost the support of the moderates and soon fizzled out.

When I moved to Madison in 1974, Paul Soglin had recently been elected mayor. Soglin, dubbed the "Red Mayor" by his detractors because of his liberal political views, had been a law student at the UW and a city alderman from the Mifflin Street area who'd been arrested in the anti-war protests. Soglin attracted national media attention. He was in his mid-thirties with long curly hair and a bushy mustache. One of the first things he did as mayor was to appoint his own police chief. When the City Council went on record opposing the war in Vietnam, conservative wags began referring to the town as "The People's Republic of Madison."

When President Nixon resigned on August 9, 1974, I was watching TV at the Pub Bar on State Street, a mile-long street that joins the campus with the Capitol. After the announcement, people poured into the streets tearing boards from buildings and making bonfires. I was standing next to a bonfire near the corner of State and Francis Streets with some other people who were smoking joints when I noticed a slim dark-haired man in shirt-sleeves standing next to me. Next to him was an older and taller man with a handlebar mustache. It was Soglin and Police Chief Cooper.

I walked over and introduced myself to Soglin.

"I just moved here and really like your city," I said.

He gave me the once over and just pointed to the bonfire.

"They just mixing it up a little?" asked Soglin.

"Yeah," I replied. "Nothing big."

He seemed satisfied. Later a newspaper reporter asked Cooper if he smelled the marijuana in the air. Cooper said no, he had a cold.

Saigon fell to the North Vietnamese on April 30, 1975. That night, Bonnie Raitt, the red-headed folk-blues artist, was performing a concert at a theater on State Street. All day long news reports told of North Vietnamese troops blitzkrieging their way through South Vietnamese lines on their way to Saigon.

About midway through the concert, Raitt stopped the show, held up a clenched fist and shouted, "Saigon has fallen. Power to the people!" The audience roared back its approval. I was swept up in the moment and joined the shouts.

In a spontaneous movement, we poured into the street and began marching around the Capitol Square. We chanted, "Ho, Ho, Ho Chi Minh . . . NLF is gonna win . . . Hey, Hey, LBJ, how many kids did you kill today?" The spirits of the war were being summoned one last time and exorcised into the crisp air of the Midwestern spring night.

4

STRIPPERS AND SNAKES

Madison – Spring 1975

WHEN I FIRST MOVED to Madison I was looking for something to renew my soul. I had quit a good job, got dumped by my fiancée and I needed a way to reconnect with people in a way that gave life meaning. I thought I'd found it when I walked into Madison General Hospital for my first day of work as a surgical orderly. The large glassed lobby with its gleaming freshly waxed floors radiated a sense of competence and the modern eight-story tower lifted my spirits.

My job involved transporting people to and from surgery. There wasn't much to learn, but I got to run around the hospital dressed like a surgeon, which garnered me admiring stares and boosted my ego. After my patients were strapped into a gurney they were helpless and looked to me for comfort. I'd tell them everything was going to be all right, like a mother talking to a scared child. I figured I was building up good karma, but I tried not to let my ego get in the way. Thirsty people needed water. Hungry people needed food. Those who suffered needed comfort. I was just the method of delivery, the truck driver of compassion.

Unfortunately, after a short time the compassion began to wear off and the patients began to annoy me. I found myself repeatedly answering the same questions.

"Excuse me doctor, but it feels like I've got cotton balls in my mouth," said one old man while I was taking him to surgery.

"Actually, I'm not a doctor. I'm an orderly," I said. "You're supposed to have a dry mouth. That's just the scopolamine in the shot they gave you. They don't want you to choke on your own saliva during surgery. Just try and relax and let the shot take effect."

"But where's my wife, doctor? I want my wife to be there. Can I see my wife?"

"I'm not a doctor; I told you that. I'm sorry but your wife will be waiting in the family room. The doctor will talk to her after you are safely out of surgery," I said, my voice rising slightly.

As we waited for the elevator the old man slipped his hand from under the sheet and held it out.

"Where are we going now doctor?"

"We're waiting for the elevator." I reached out and gently held his hand. It was as cold as death.

The elevator doors opened and I took him upstairs to surgery. If he wanted to think I was a doctor, it was OK with me. I could play the game and for those few minutes I could feel that I was someone who was respected in a society that seemed to value personal achievement over everything.

Patients had lots of questions about their surgery, but we couldn't answer them because it wasn't our job. We weren't nurses aids, we were transporters — the deck apes of surgery. On a bad day I'd slam the empty carts against the wall, knocking monotonous, mind-numbing questions from the brains of imaginary patients. While I viewed the job as a sort of a spiritual exercise when I started, my ego soon reasserted itself and I returned to being pushed and pulled by my desires. Although people always will have desires, Ram Dass taught us not to identify with them and eventually they would fall away. I had failed the exercise. I was left without purpose, drawn to anything that made me feel good for the moment.

One day after work I was walking down State Street, identifying with a dull throbbing in my head, the beginning migraine headache. Coming toward me were Sandy and Jackie, two housekeepers I knew from the hospital.

Sandy was a tall homely brunette with large breasts and a nice figure while Jackie was short and plump with a pretty face. A couple weeks earlier I had run into Sandy at a biker bar on the East Side. I recognized her from the hospital and after a little conversation we began to dance in a small room off the main bar with a pool table and a juke box. She was wearing a gauzy semi-transparent tunic and when we danced she set me on fire when I felt her nipples rubbing against my chest. After the dance I asked her over to my place, but she said she couldn't go because she had a biker boyfriend who frequented the bar and was afraid he would find out. I backed off but remained turned on by the dangerous eroticism of the situation.

When I saw her on the street the memory of that encounter flashed back through my mind like a shot of nirvana.

"Hey, Richard, what's happening," said Sandy. They both laughed and walked me down the street backwards as if they were kidnapping me.

"I'm just gettin' off work," I said. "Where's the party?"

I stopped and turned around, adjusting the brim of my hat.

"Why don't you come over," said Sandy. She came in closer and whispered in my ear with mock confidentiality, "We've got some Colombian."

I gave her a little squeeze and winked. The gold-colored marijuana from Colombia was known for its potency. It sold for $30 an ounce, a little rich for my blood, but a couple tokes and you were flying.

"Well, I was going to run some errands," I said, trying to play it cool, "but I can make an exception in this case."

We took Jackie's car to a small house on the west side of town. The girls brought out a pipe and stuffed it with marijuana. As the stereo blasted out country-rock songs from a Marshall Tucker Band album, we passed the pipe around and got high.

"Nice house," I yelled to Jackie above the blaring stereo.

"What?"

"Nice house," I said, taking a hit off the pipe. I passed it to her.

She sucked in some smoke, and then exhaled. "What about your house?"

"My house? Whadaya mean?" I was confused. I could barely hear her above music.

"You said something about your house."

"No . . . no. Not my house, this house."

"So what about this house?"

"It's nice . . . nice . . . you know, a nice house."

"Oh, yeah. Actually it's not my house. It's Sandy's house."

Jackie handed me the pipe, but I put it on the table. Sandy was gone.

"Where's Sandy?" I yelled as the guitar solo from *Born a Traveling Man* was ending.

"We don't have any candy," said Jackie.

I gave up trying to communicate, leaned back into the beanbag chair and waited until the song was over. When Jackie got up to go to the bathroom I started looking for Sandy and found her lying on a bed in the next room facing the wall. Biker boyfriend or not, I couldn't pass up a chance like this.

I slipped into her bed and cuddled up next to her. She turned toward me and said, "What are you doing in my bed?"

"It's not nice to desert your guests," I said. "Just thought I'd come in and keep you company."

I ran my fingers down her back and then around to her breasts.

"Mmmm . . . that feels good," she purred. She turned around, hooked her leg around my waist and after a few minutes we yanked off our clothes and I began sucking on her erect nipples. She moaned and drew me inside of her. She came first and then, as I was nearing my climax, the phone rang.

"Don't answer, I'm almost there," I cried in desperation. I came after the seventh ring. Sandy pushed me aside, sprang from the bed and picked up the receiver. Her boyfriend was on the other end.

"No, everything is all right, honey" I heard her say. "The stereo was just really loud."

As I lay exhausted on her bed, she dressed quickly and left. Jackie gave me a ride back to State Street and dropped me off where they had "abducted" me. I still had a headache.

A couple weeks later, I was at a strip joint called the Dangle Lounge. The club was across from the State Capitol in the heart of a block of cheesy bars. I paid three dollars to get in, then waited while my eyes adjusted to the dark. Inside was a long, narrow room with a bar. Behind the bar was a small stage bathed in red light filtered through heavy clouds of cigarette smoke. The room was crowded. Rock music blared from two speakers on either side of the stage and a naked dancer slithered around with a boa constrictor.

I elbowed my way to the bar and bought a bottle of beer. The dancer was bent slightly backward clasping a python between her thighs, its head slowly curling above like Eve and the serpent without Adam. My eyes scanned the crowd consisting of beefy conventioneers from a banker's meeting in town. But wait! What's this guy in a white turban doing here? I moved closer. It was Ken-Adi.

I poked him in the side. "What's a nice boy like you doing in a place like this?" I asked.

"Oh, hi Richard. I'm watching my girlfriend."

My eyes darted to the stage where the dancer was putting the head of the snake into her mouth.

My potential guru? In a strip joint? Going with a stripper? Ram Dass wrote that gurus are often like ordinary people. They are just more in touch with cosmic awareness. I offered to buy him a beer, but he said no. He didn't drink. I was a little relieved.

After the lounge closed we went outside and I met his girlfriend, Sue. On stage she was a hot, young, redhead with long sensuous legs, voluptuous breasts, and sultry eyes. Here, out on the street, she was a short, average-looking girl with her hair tied back wearing coke-bottle glasses.

Sue said she only worked two shows a day, but made over $150 a week, which was enough to live on. I gave them a ride back to their house on Williamson Street. Soon I would be taking a much longer ride with Ken-Adi.

5
A VISIT FROM MY MOTHER
Madison – Summer 1975

IN MAY THE FARMER'S MARKET opened on the Capitol Square and hundreds of local growers brought in bouquets of spring flowers, scallions, greenhouse parsley, quarts of honey and maple syrup. People with pale skin and floppy hats strolled around the Square admiring the large yellow and red clusters of tulips planted on the lawn surrounding the Capitol. The city flushed its fire hydrants, sending torrents of water racing around curbs. As she had done every year, Mother Nature transformed Wisconsin into a warm and hospitable place.

With the change of seasons I began to feel closed in at the hospital and soon lost interest in my job. Sometimes I got high before I came to work. As my attitude began to deteriorate, I received negative performance evaluations and knew my time as an OR transporter was coming to an end.

Later that summer I ran into Ken-Adi on the street. He wanted to take some massage courses in San Francisco and asked me to go with him. I jumped at the chance for an adventure. I needed to get the cobwebs out of my mind and stop squeezing time into small segments of patient pick-ups and drop-offs. I also wanted to find out more about Ken-Adi.

Was he my connection to enlightenment or just another lost soul? On the way back I wanted to stop in Fort Collins, Colorado and see Dave Crum, the person who first got me interested in Ram Dass. Dave was applying for graduate school in anthropology at Colorado State and seemed to have his life in order, while mine was floundering. Perhaps he could help me find my way.

I gave the hospital two weeks notice and began to make travel plans.

I suggested we hitch because my beater car would never survive the trip. I had taken several hitchhiking trips in the past, although never with someone else. Ken-Adi hadn't done much hitching, but agreed to give it a try.

At the same time, my mother decided to come to Wisconsin to visit some relatives and check up on her wayward son. Her timing was terrible but I decided to make the best of it.

My mother, Marjory, had grown up with her older sister during the Depression in the small central Wisconsin farming community of Westfield. Dairy farming was a hard life, and her mother wanted none of it for her daughters. She sent them both to college and thought that with an education they would be able to make something of their lives. My mother expected the same for me.

A week before my trip with Ken-Adi, my mother arrived. I didn't have much room in my small apartment, so she stayed at a hotel. In the morning she took a cab to my place, which was located in the rear of a three-flat on East Johnson Street. She was average height, slim with reddish-brown hair, and wore a blazer with slacks.

"Hi, Mom," I said, giving her a hug.

"My goodness, look at your hair," she said. "When are you going to get it cut?"

"I'm not," I said, staking out my own territory early.

"Come on in," I said, leading her up the stairs to my tiny living room. My small apartment was furnished with a stuffed chair and an old couch covered with a Navajo blanket. In the corner was a bookcase with a golden plaster replica of Buddha holding a stick of incense.

"I know the apartment is small, but I'm only paying $120 a month for it," I said, immediately annoyed with myself because it sounded like I was apologizing.

"It's very nice," she said flatly. She put her purse on the floor next to the chair and sat down facing the Buddha.

"So, aren't you going to ask me how I am?" she said.

"How are you?"

"I'm fine. I had a very good sleep at the Concourse Hotel. It's very nice. Of course I would rather have stayed with my son, but that's all right. Maybe some day you will have a house of your own I can visit."

"So," she went on, "I heard from Bette that you quit your job at the hospital."

Suddenly the hate flashed up inside of me and I let a little leak out. "Yeah, well, things were gettin' kinda heavy there," I said, lapsing into my hippie street slang. "I mean, you know, everyone started to get on my nerves."

"I really don't know why you were working there in the first place," she said. "Maybe it was just because your father worked as an orderly while he was thinking of going to medical school."

"I thought I'd see what working in a hospital was like. I was thinking of getting into the medical field." We had discussed this on the phone earlier.

"Well, it's your life," she said. "What about journalism? You already went to school for that. Why don't you give that another try?"

My heart began thumping, and a flash of warmth ran up the sides of my neck as I remembered the last serious attempt I made at getting a reporting job two years earlier. I was sitting in the editor's office at Colorado Springs Sun. He had just offered me a job.

"What are your salary requirements?" he asked. Having gotten $130 a week at my previous job, I said, "I was thinking of $150 a week."

The managing editor looked at the editor, and they both smiled at each other with thin-pursed lips as if they were sharing a private joke. "Well, that's considerably more than we pay," he said.

I was stunned and mumbled something about that being insufficient. The next morning I hitchhiked back to Chicago with two dollars in my pocket. They didn't want writers; they wanted indentured servants.

"There are no jobs up here in journalism. I checked when I first moved. You know that."

"What if I told you there was a job opening in Milwaukee working with John?" She surprised me.

My cousin John had a motel travel guide franchise there. "Doin' what?"

"He needs some help with his magazine. It would be a start."

"I'm goin' out West with a buddy of mine."

Her eyes widened. "You're going to do what?" She looked out the window, biting her lip, and then turned back to me.

"How are you going to get there? With that piece of junk you're driving?"

"We're gonna hitch it."

She clenched the arms of her chair and pulled herself forward. "I'm offering you a chance to straighten out your life and you're going to hitchhike?" She said the word "hitchhike" like it was a dead cockroach she was picking up with a tweezers. "Out West? You're thirty years old. You're not a teenager anymore. When are you ever going to grow up and become a responsible person? I'm thoroughly disgusted with you."

"I don't give a shit about John and his magazine," I shouted back. I got up and went into the kitchen. I took a breath and returned to the living room.

"Look, I'm trying to get things together. Maybe I can get a job at the hospital when I get back. I'm just taking a little vacation."

"I thought you didn't like hospital work. They were giving you 'hassles.'" She said "hassles" in a whiny, singsong voice, mocking me.

"Look, I don't want to discuss it anymore," I said, chopping the air with both my hands. "I'm trying . . . to do . . . what I feel . . . is right . . . not . . . what you . . . think I should do."

"All I want is what's best for you," she said. "I think you're making a big mistake."

And there she left it, lying on my living room floor — the "big mistake" that would one day consume me. Once my head was in its jaws, my last thought would be that I had a mother who only wanted the best for me.

"I'll call you a cab," I said.

We made small talk. When the taxi arrived she got up, grabbed her purse and I gave her a little hug.

She smiled. "Let's have breakfast together at the hotel before I leave. My treat."

"Sounds great," I said.

After she left I slumped into my armchair and stared at the Buddha. Was I just hitching out west to piss her off? I didn't think so, but with her I was never sure of my motivations.

PART TWO
THE TRIP WEST

6
THE PRIMAL SCREAM
Chicago 1970-1973

THE FOLLOWING DAY my mother left for home and I resumed planning for the trip. I had second thoughts about hitching all the way to California with Ken-Adi because it was always more difficult getting a ride with two people.

Before we left Madison I got a copy of the *Chicago Tribune* and checked the classifieds under "Travel Opportunities." We were in luck. There were several ads for drivers to deliver cars from agencies in Chicago to points west.

Sue offered us a ride to Chicago. On a warm, muggy day in early August, we threw our packs in her beat-up Chevy station wagon and headed out.

As we drove south, long rows of sweet corn stretched up and over the gently rolling hills, their tall green stalks and yellow tassels indicating they were ready for harvest. In the eastern sky, a huge thunderhead formed. High winds swept its bulbous crown, creating a wispy anvil. Nearing the Illinois border, we descended into a valley where the Rock River cut a sharp gorge in the farmland. Little cottages and boats dotted the shore, creating a separate world of river life, within the rural landscape. Beyond the river were more large, flat expanses of cornfields and dairy farms.

When we entered the Illinois Tollway the road opened up to four lanes, then curved southeast and ran smack into urban sprawl and the gray-brown haze of Chicago.

Memories of my fiancée started coming back. We passed the Old Orchard Shopping Center where she had helped me pick out a sport coat. The names of suburbs where I delivered pizza after we'd broken up flashed by — Evanston, Willamette, Winnetka, Schaumburg, and Skokie. Her house was in Skokie and part of me wanted to see her again. Why couldn't I forget her? It had been two years.

I met Linda in 1970, shortly after I left the Navy and returned to college. I was studying journalism at Columbia College, a small private college in downtown Chicago. A mutual friend of ours had given me her phone number. I called her and she asked me to stop by for a visit.

On a brisk afternoon in early October I drove my Volkswagen Bug to her house in Skokie, a trip that would become pivotal in my life. I pulled up across from a comfortable-looking one-story ranch house east of the interstate where she lived with her family. A young woman with long brown hair was walking a black and white Cocker Spaniel beneath the trees, which were starting to change colors. I got out of the car.

She stared at me a moment and said, "Are you Richard?"

"You must be Linda," I said walking over to her. She was slim and wore bell-bottom jeans and an ox-colored suede coat.

"Did you have any trouble finding the house?" she asked. "A lot of people think it's on the other side of the interstate."

"No problem."

We made small talk as we waited for her dog to do its business, then went inside her house. She hung our jackets in the closet and we sat down at a breakfast nook in the kitchen, where a teakettle was heating up on the stove.

"So where is the rest of your family?" I asked.

"My father is at work. He's a pharmacist and we have a drug store near Oak Park," she said. The kettle began to whistle.

"Tea feels so nice and warm on a cold day."

She got up and removed the kettle from the stove.

"Tea?" she asked.

"Yes, please."

She poured the hot water into two cups, put two teabags in, then set the cups on the table.

"My mother works as a receptionist at Lyman Industries," she continued. "It's an electronics manufacturer."

"I think you told me on the phone that you have three brothers."

"Two," she said. "Tom is at the University of Chicago studying math and Sammy is a junior in high school. Everyone usually gets home around six."

I relaxed a little. At least we'd have some time to visit before her family arrived.

The scene was very familiar. I'd grown up in a similar neighborhood in Miami. When I left home I'd given up suburbia for the Navy, college, and then an apartment on the North Side of Chicago. Since then I had adopted a scornful attitude about the 'burbs as a place where people were isolated from the world and only cared about maintaining a bourgeois standard of living.

"On the phone you said you were going to school in Iowa," I said.

Linda took a sip of tea. "Would you like some sugar?"

"No, I'm all right," I said, waiting for a reply.

"Do you want some honey?" she pushed an earthenware container with a wooden dipper in front of me.

I opened the container, pulled out the stick, and slowly dripped some thick honey into my tea, holding it there until the last drop broke loose.

I tried again. "So . . . you were in college in Iowa?"

Linda took a deep breath and began stirring her tea briskly. "A friend of mine was going there, so I decided to give it a try."

"Why aren't you there anymore?"

"I had some problems," she began. "It's good to talk about it . . . I guess, even though I'm not sure exactly why it happened."

"Hey, if you don't want to talk about it, that's fine with me."

"Thanks, but really it helps, especially if we're going to be friends," she said. "One day just before a test I started to have trouble breathing. I tried to ignore it, but I couldn't. Finally I passed out and they took me to the hospital. The doctors ran some tests and everything checked out okay, so I rested for a day and then tried going back to classes. A week later the same thing happened. I got so that I didn't even want to leave the dorm. It was awful."

"I'm sorry," I said. "I didn't want to make you feel uncomfortable."

"I'm getting better now," she said and smiled. "Have you heard George Harrison's new album, *All Things Must Pass*? I've been playing it a lot. He's such a spiritual person. It gives me a lot of comfort."

"I didn't know he recorded anything since the Beatles broke up," I said.

"Let's go to my room. I'll play it for you," said Linda. She took our cups up a short flight of stairs and into her dimly lit bedroom where she had a small bed, a rocking chair and her stereo. An easel and some oil paintings were stacked in a corner.

She put the cups on a small table and picked up an album with a picture of Harrison on the cover sporting a long, gray beard and a hat. He was sitting on a chair in the middle of a field surrounded by several elves lying on the ground looking up at him.

"Sit down," said Linda, gesturing to the rocker.

I lowered myself into the rocking chair as Linda placed the needle on the record, and then sat on her bed. I leaned back in the chair and began to rock back and forth slowly.

The music was an eclectic blend of music from India combined with American country, rock & roll, and blues. Linda sat against the wall with her arms around her legs mouthing the words to the songs.

Her brown eyes were warm and clear and focused above my head as Harrison sang the words to *My Sweet Lord*.

> *I really want to see you*
> *Really want to see you, lord*
> *Really want to see you, lord*
> *But it takes so long, my lord.*
> (chorus) *Hare Krishna, Hare Rama,*
> *Rama Rama, Krishna Krishna. . . .*

Tears began to form in her eyes. More deeply spiritual songs followed. Some were devotional and romantic, while others were a kaleidoscope of sounds. When Harrison sang *What Is Life*, I began singing along with Linda.

> *Tell me, what is my life without your love.*
> *Tell me who am I without you, by my side.*

She looked at me and smiled. Song after song, the lyrics reflected a spiritual yearning. After we listened to both sides she said, "Well, there it is; how did you like it?"

"Great," I said. She didn't say anything so I said, "Really, it was great. I like it a lot."

"I don't know what I'd do without music," she said. "Music is like the soul of life revealed as sound. Without it I don't think I'd have the desire to keep on living."

"Yeah . . . I really like it too. It's a good thing Harrison broke with the Beatles," I said.

We had some more tea and talked about her painting. Linda painted dark canvases of swirling colors and abstract forms. When she dropped out of school she was majoring in art and hoped to pick it back up when she felt better. It was getting dark when her parents got home. Her father was a big, good-natured man in his late fifties who spoke in a loud voice. After we said hello he retired to the living room with his newspaper. Her mother was a well-dressed suburban matron with graying hair and a very friendly demeanor. I had some homework to do and it was getting late, so we said good-bye and I invited her to stop by my apartment sometime.

On the drive back to my apartment I was excited about having met Linda. She was obviously a very beautiful and sensitive person and I looked forward to our next meeting, although I wondered what caused her breathing difficulties.

We started dating and soon she began to tell me about her breathing problems, a type of panic disorder. I gladly accepted the role of her comforter and confidante. Sometimes she stopped in at my apartment after her group therapy sessions. Often she fell into my arms at the door, crying softly. I caressed her and told her she would be OK. We fell in love. Soon Linda's parents began inviting me over for dinner and treating me like family. I began to envision a future with her. However, as our intimacy deepened, so did our problems.

About six months after Linda and I met, we were at a restaurant after seeing the movie *Death in Venice*. The film, based on the novella by Thomas Mann, was about an aging German professor who is disillusioned with the sterile quality of his life. He goes to Venice and sees a boy who is the embodiment of his lost passion. He tries to make himself look more attractive to the boy, but only succeeds in appearing more grotesque. I thought the plot was silly.

Linda sat across from me at the table. "Wow, that was a weird movie," I said.

"What do you mean, weird?" asked Linda. "I thought it was amazing."

"The main character . . . what was his name?"

"Gustave."

"Yeah, here's Gustave, following this young kid around . . . pretty weird."

"He wasn't just following him around," Linda said, raising her voice. "He was trying to recapture his youth."

"In Chicago we call people like that stalkers," I said.

The waitress came with menus. I ordered coffee and Linda ordered some tea.

"You're missing the point," said Linda. "Here's a man who has lived a very controlled, boring life and he's spiritually empty. He goes to Venice and he's looking for some way to get back in touch with his feelings. He wants to feel passionate about something, anything. He sees this beautiful young man, boy, whatever, and feels something that is genuine."

"OK. I get that, but he's living in a fantasy world. He's got zero chance of ever having a relationship with the boy because he's with his parents."

The waitress returned with our drinks. I added cream to my coffee while Linda put some sugar in her tea and stirred.

"Why do you have to be so practical all the time? Can't you just appreciate the beauty of feelings?"

Oh, shit, I thought, here it comes . . . I'm going to have to talk about feelings again.

"I appreciate feelings." I said. "I just don't think a man following a boy around is something I want to pay money to see."

"It's not the money, Richard. I think you're just afraid of feelings. It's becoming very clear. All you can think about are the objective facts. Maybe it's the journalism. I really don't know."

"Well . . . that's true. When I write a newspaper story I've gotta keep my feelings out of it."

"I understand that," said Linda, drawing out the "a" sound in "that." "You carry it over into everything. When we went to the Renoir exhibit last month you said it was 'nice.' Didn't that speak to anything deeper in you? It did for me. But I didn't have anyone to share that with."

"Sorry."

Linda was on a roll. "And now this movie and the music . . . I just lost myself in the music. It was ecstasy. How could you not be moved by that?"

I felt my psyche retreating behind a concrete bunker. I didn't like talking about feelings. I felt them . . . I reacted to things with them . . . and that was it. Why talk about them? I loved Linda, I made love to her, I told her I loved her . . . what more did she want? Yet, whenever I didn't feel the required depth of emotion I was "insensitive." That pissed me off. "Stay the fuck outta my mind," I wanted to yell. "You're sucking me dry." But I couldn't let that happen because she would see my ugly side and be repulsed.

I took a breath and swallowed, forcing the rage back down my throat. Was there something wrong with me? Maybe I had repressed my feelings for years. Slowly I began to sense a vague, almost forgotten place in my mind where music, art, and beauty once ruled my spirit. I recalled myself as a child looking up at my phonograph as Spike Jones razzmatazz music blared from the speaker and I danced joyously around the floor on the balls of my feet.

Suddenly I felt tired. I slumped forward and looked at Linda. Her warm brown eyes pleaded for understanding. She was so beautiful. "I'm sorry," is all I could say.

"Richard," she said with a note of sympathy in her voice, "I just can't live like this. I need a relationship where I can share my passions with another person, a relationship that's spiritually rewarding."

Linda was slipping away. I loved her so much. I had to say something to stop her. "Look, I'm trying to change." I said. "I know it's hard for you, but it's hard for me, too. I'm trying. That's all I can do."

Linda took my hand. "I just want us to stay together. I want our love to grow. Is that asking too much?"

I smiled and wiped a tear from my eye. "No, it isn't. I can do it. I can get in touch with my spirit. I know I can."

And so my spiritual quest began, in a desperate attempt to save a doomed relationship.

Linda grew more confident in herself after she resumed her art courses and enrolled in a college program. While she concentrated on expressing feelings on canvas, I studied how to eliminate expressing mine in newspaper stories. In spite of our best efforts, sharing and intimacy continued to be a problem.

I graduated from college in June of 1972. In October I got a job on a small newspaper in LaPorte, Indiana, seventy miles east of Chicago. Linda stayed behind to finish school. I hoped to work in Indiana for a year and then get a job in the Chicago area. Maybe then we could get married.

During the first few months of my job I drove in to see her every weekend, but as the months wore on, our visits became less frequent. She developed her own circle of art friends and soon the roles reversed. Now she needed more space while I needed more intimacy. I couldn't bear the thought of living without her.

I quit my job and moved back to Chicago. We decided to make one last attempt to save the relationship by getting an apartment together.

I got a job delivering pizza and slept on a ex-college buddy's couch. Soon, however, Linda had second thoughts about living with me. She needed time to "get her head together" and moved in with a girlfriend. We went for couple's counseling and I joined a therapy group.

Just before Thanksgiving in 1973 the situation came to a head. We had plans to see the J. Geils Band at a downtown club. When I got to her friend's apartment, she was sitting at a coffee table in the living room having a cup of tea, still dressed in her bathrobe.

"What are you doing in your robe?" I asked. "We're going to be late."

She remained seated, avoiding eye contact.

I took off my sport coat and hung it on the back of a kitchen chair. I was losing my patience, yet I didn't want to upset her. My future hung on her thread of indifference. A wave of anger rose, but I fought it down. I walked back into the living room where she sat, staring into her cup. I tried to sound friendly as I spoke.

"Well, I . . . ah . . . I want to ask you something." Here it goes. "When do you think you'll be ready to get an apartment with me?"

"I don't know," she answered flatly.

I took a deep breath. "Look Linda," I said. "I quit my job, moved to Evanston, and have been living on Neil's couch for three weeks waiting for you to make up your mind. I'm trying to give you enough time to get it together, but I just want to know what the hell I'm supposed to do."

Linda looked up from her cup, glanced at my face and said, "That's your problem."

I was stunned; then I began to tremble. Linda remained seated, staring at the wall. My anger exploded. "You fucking bitch, you god damn fucking bitch," I shouted waving my arms wildly. I moved toward her, but stopped. What was I doing? I turned around, grabbed my coat and left, slamming the door so hard it shook the walls of the building. I ran down the stairs and jumped into my car.

Is this really happening? The muscles in my body began to twitch and my stomach churned as my life unraveled before my eyes.

I drove to Neil's in Evanston and banged on the side door. Neil let me in. I was still shaking.

"What happened?" he asked.

I leaned against the kitchen wall, held my head in my hands, and tried not to cry. "I gotta get out of town, Linda . . . we broke . . . up. How much money you got?"

Neil emptied his pockets on the table. He had six dollars and thirty-five cents. I took it and left for Bloomington, Indiana, where my sister Sandra attended college. After I had been there a couple days, I wrote Linda a brief letter saying that I realized our relationship was over.

When I got back to Chicago two weeks later, I returned to the therapy group. The group met at an apartment in trendy Lincoln Park and was led by a stocky, middle-aged therapist named Allen Jacobs. My main problem was that I couldn't sleep much or concentrate. I needed heavy medicine. I needed primal scream.

Allen and his co-therapist, a thin, middle-aged woman with short, black hair, sat with group members in a circle. The primal scream work was done on a mat in the middle of the circle, but group members had to ask for it.

Allen began the meeting, as usual, by discussing anything that came to his mind. The ground rules were that if someone wanted to discuss their problems, they had to interrupt him. That way no one was forced to do anything.

"Wow, I've got something special to tell you this week," began Allen. "I've been appointed to head the National Transactional Analysis Convention." He was beaming. Everyone congratulated him. "I didn't think I'd be chosen. It's a real honor. I've been working on it every year and I almost thought . . ."

"Allen," I interrupted, "I want to do some mat work. I just broke up with Linda. Maybe you heard."

"Yes, she called and told me last week. I was sorry to hear that." He motioned to his assistant. "All right, Kathy?"

Kathy spread a mat on the floor in the center of our circle.

"Come here and lie down, Rich," she said.

I got up and lay down on the mat. Kathy knelt beside me and looked into my eyes.

"Now remember, maintain eye contact with me. I don't want you getting lost," she said.

I was familiar with the procedure, having watched other group members go through it.

"Okay," I said.

Kathy placed pillows under my feet, arms and head. I felt awkward and wondered, can I really do this?

"Now, begin turning your head from side to side, raise your arms to the ceiling and alternate bringing them down on the pillows," she said.

I began. Thud. I hit one pillow with my right hand, brought it back up, then hit the other pillow with my left hand. Thud.

"Turn your head," she said. Allen observed from a distance.

I hit the pillows again, this time turning my head to the left when I brought my right hand down and vice versa.

"Good, "said Kathy. "Now each time you turn your head, exhale."

I got into the rhythm. Turn, exhale, slam. Turn, exhale, slam. I still felt silly and became a bit light-headed.

"What do you want to tell Linda?" asked Kathy.

I wanted to tell her lots of things. But most of all I wanted to hurt her. I wanted to make sure she felt my pain, but I wasn't sure how to express it. OK, here it goes.

"God damn you, Linda," I said without much feeling.

"Louder," urged Kathy.

"God damn you, Linda," I shouted.

"Come on, you must be more pissed off than that," she said. "Tell the bitch exactly what you think of her."

Suddenly a hot ball of hate rose from deep within me.

"God damn you, you fucking cunt," I screamed and attacked the pillows.

"Look into my eyes," reminded Kathy.

"God damn you, you fucking, worthless cunt!" The shouts became shrieks as I flailed away at the pillows. I repeated the cries over and over again. Finally I arched my back, jerked my body upward, poured out my last curse and fell limp — exhausted. I laughed and laughed, wiped the tears from my eyes and felt better than I had for months.

While the primal scream relieved a pent-up anger, it didn't remove the sadness from my heart.

I went home for Christmas then drove back to Chicago. I forgot about getting a job in journalism and began delivering pizza. Still, I felt Linda's presence and needed closure. I called her at home and we agreed to meet.

On a cold, blustery day in late December, I climbed into my car and drove to her house in Skokie. I had tried to build a wall between us. Now that barrier was about to be tested. I was terrified.

My tires crunched on the hard-packed snow and ice. Even though the heater wasn't working well, I broke out in a sweat. I pulled into the driveway of her house and shut off the motor. This is it, I thought. No turning back now.

I entered the porch where my belongings were stacked in boxes against the wall. I knocked on the door, took a breath and tried to relax. There was no response. I knocked again. What would happen when I saw her? I could give her a friendly hug and make some small talk, be cordial, yet restrained. That was the best approach. Keep it as unemotional as possible. I didn't want a repeat of our last meeting. Frozen wisps of my breath vanished in front of her yellow porch light. Finally I heard her voice coming from the far side of the kitchen.

"Come on in."

I opened the door. She was standing across the room wearing a pink, quilted robe. She looked heavier and wasn't wearing any makeup. Her long, voluptuous, auburn hair had been cut back into a mid-sixties Monkees' style. She looked like a nun.

"You look different," I said.

"So do you," she answered.

We stared at each other for a moment.

"I don't want to get too close because I've got a cold," she said.

That was just fine with me. I was glad she wasn't so close and glad she was fat and pale. I slowly pushed the door shut behind me and sat down on a chair next to the breakfast table, the same table where I had eaten so many times with her family. Steady now. Don't let your thoughts run amok. I couldn't think of anything to say. I felt awkward in my heavy boots and jacket, but I didn't want to take off my armor. A sob began to grow in my throat, but I choked it off.

"It's pretty cold out there," I ventured.

"I know, I've had a cold for a week now."

She walked to the stove and picked up a pot of boiling water. "Do you want some tea?"

"Sure," I said.

She brought out two saucers and two teacups and placed them on the table as she had done the first day we met. Then she poured the hot water into them and brought two teabags from the cupboard.

I unbuttoned my pea coat and felt more at ease. Her brown eyes met mine, and I let a little love flow back into my heart. We had shared a lot. No reason to treat her like a stranger. I told her the past few weeks had been tough. She said it had been difficult for her, too. Gradually we talked ourselves back to the night we broke up.

"You know," I said, "at first I thought we might get back together, but the more I thought about it, the more I could see that it was over."

"I know," she said, biting her lip. "I thought the same thing, but you're right. I was a mess for a while. I didn't go outside. I was in a fog. And that door. It kept slamming in my head."

I smiled. "Good, that's what I wanted." She took no offense.

"I keep wanting to say 'I'm sorry'," she said.

"That's okay. It couldn't have been any other way."

Then suddenly, it seemed that everything had been said.

I got up from the table. "I hope your mother doesn't mind all my stuff on the porch. I'll be getting an apartment pretty soon," I said, buttoning my coat.

Linda walked me to the door. When I turned around to say good-bye we were almost touching, so I gave her a hug and kissed her on the forehead.

"I'll let you know when I'm ready to move," I said.

As the door closed, so did a phase of my life. What had begun three years earlier with such hope, ended in bitter disappointment. Yet, I had survived. Outside, a bright winter sun shone on the crisp, white snow covering the lawn. My boots squeaked as I walked to my car. I opened the door, sat down on a cold, hard seat and started the engine. The motor coughed and began knocking. When the idle began to even out I backed up slowly from the driveway, glancing at Linda's picture window. I couldn't see inside because the frost obscured my view. That was okay. I was free. But free to do what?

7

Gunga Din

Chicago – Summer 1975

LINDA'S HOUSE was within view of the expressway, just south of the Touhy exit. Or was it north of the Touhy exit? Was that the park on her corner? Trees blocked the line of sight and in a flash my past receded in the rearview mirror. A part of me still wanted to go home to Linda.

The exits quickly came and went — Foster, Irving Park, Belmont. We continued south. Tired, sweating commuters bunched up along the El tracks, which ran down the center of the expressway. Traffic in the northbound lanes started backing up. Buses and semis belched their black diesel fumes into the oppressively hot, humid air.

We exited the expressway onto Ohio Street and made our way toward the delivery agency, which was housed in a dirty, red, brick building downtown. Ken-Adi jumped out and ran upstairs while Sue and I parked. She waited in the car while I carried our backpacks up a long flight of stairs to the AAA Drive-Away Agency. A fat, bald little man with a cigar was sitting behind a desk.

"Excuse me," I said. He looked up. "Did a guy in a white turban just come in here?"

"Oh, yeah, you mean Gunga Din?" he said. He led me into a back room where Ken-Adi was being fingerprinted.

"Oh, hi Richard," he said when I walked in. "I've got the car."

We filled out some forms and put down a $75 deposit. The forms asked for references, so we gave them Sue's name and address. None of the information was verified. We could have been car thieves. The little fat man gave us the keys to a 1972 Ford station wagon to deliver to Wichita, Kansas within forty-eight hours.

We both kissed Sue good-bye, then headed for the tourist mecca of Old Town, just north of the loop. As we browsed through a souvenir store one of the Indian shopkeepers, a heavy-set man with a black spot on his forehead, offered Ken-Adi a cigarette. Not being a smoker, he refused. We continued browsing and again the shopkeeper returned, this time with a bottle of Coca-Cola. Again Ken-Adi refused the man's hospitality. I was puzzled by the man's generosity until I remembered something I read from Ram Dass' *Be Here Now*. In the Hindu tradition, giving a gift to a holy man brought the giver good luck. Well, I'll be damned, I thought. If real Hindus think Ken-Adi is a holy man, then maybe he is my guru after all.

We left Chicago before sunset and drove all night, south on I-55 through flat Illinois farmland, then west on I-70 toward a place where my life had begun to unravel ten years earlier.

8
A FATHER'S PLEA
Missouri – 1965

I HAD SPENT one disappointing year at the University of Missouri in Columbia before flunking out and joining the Navy.

The university had an excellent reputation for journalism so I transferred there in 1965 after two years of junior college in Miami.

The catch was that before I could take any journalism courses I had to pass two semesters of a foreign language. I had tried Spanish and German in junior college, but had done poorly in both. However, I was determined to give it another try at Missouri.

Shortly after my dad dropped me off at the dorm, he sent me a letter. He contrasted me with a "colored GI" he picked up while hitchhiking, who was going to Vietnam. "You and this boy, Robbie Styles, became poignant symbols," he wrote. "Dick: blond, ivory tower environment, last seen in the bright sunlight, posh living quarters and a future that smiles. Robbie Styles: Black, riding with me at night through heavy fog, facing a grim future and possible death . . . I didn't tell him about you." Maybe he didn't tell Robbie Styles about me because he didn't want to make him feel bad, but I think there was something else going on.

For a number of years there had been a tension between my father and me. It began one summer in my early teens when he was away from home for a long stretch selling land. I was at a point in my life when I needed fathering and I missed him desperately. When the ache in my heart became too much to bear, the loneliness turned into resentment and then anger. I felt abandoned, but it was really me who abandoned him. When he returned, there was an emotional chasm between us. We each retreated to our separate spaces — he struggled to make money and I turned toward my friends for support.

The first semester at the University of Missouri I took a full schedule including Spanish. To keep my spirits up, I'd stroll by the School of Journalism. I was drawn to the weathered gray stone exterior and heavy ornate doors because it was a repository for all the vital knowledge I needed to become a successful journalist. Sometimes I would pull the doors open and go inside to study the map of the world.

Colored pins in a world map indicated places where graduates were working. Next to the map was a plaque listing the names of famous graduates. After staring at the map I'd walk by the modern, one-story structure housing *The Missourian*, a student-run daily newspaper. My fingers were itchin' to bang out stories at *The Missourian*. That's really all I wanted to do.

As the semester dragged on with no journalism courses in my schedule, I lost interest in most of my classes and flunked the first semester of Spanish. For my second semester I tried Latin because an advisor told me that it was mostly a written language. My advisor thought it would be easier because I wouldn't have to speak it, but by mid-term I was flunking that, too. The maddening complexities of word conjugations sent my brain into shock. I was afraid I was going to flunk out. For the first time in my life I seriously considered joining the military.

Instead of going home to see my family for spring break I headed to Ft. Lauderdale. I needed time to relax and forget about my problems. My dad didn't know what to do with me. On March 26, 1966, he expressed his frustration in a letter, underlining key words.

He began with an apology.

We feel we should have left Miami several years ago, before you absorbed too much of the fun virus that seems to have directed your behavior pattern. Regardless of your future plans, you have about two months left to discipline yourself and put forth that <u>extra effort</u> to gain college credits with respectable grades. If some of your difficulty is due to bad or inadequate parental influence, we are sorry, but don't give up.

Next he tried to rally me to action.

Expect <u>more</u> of <u>yourself</u> and set about doing what you <u>know</u> you must do . . . I wish you would be aggressive and <u>hire</u> a <u>Latin tutor</u> with the understanding that if you get a "C" or even pass Latin, he will be given a cash bonus. That sort of thing is done in business to get the job done. Why can't a student do it?

Then he tried an appeal to my emotion.

Why don't you get <u>mad</u> and <u>make things</u> happen? No matter how tough the job seems to you <u>now</u>, it's possible to create a *new surge of energy and determination and put on a strong finish. What can I do to build a fire under you?*

Finally he concluded by hinting at the obvious.

Join the service if you wish, but make this semester a phase of your life where you won a tough battle! Sacrifice and suffer, but do the job you don't want to admit you must do.

His sales pitch came too late. I think he just wanted to reassure himself that he had given me his best try.

The only course I cared about was a one-credit class called The American Mountain Man, taught by a small, eighty-year-old gnome of a man with long, silver-white hair named John Neidhardt. As a young man, Neidhardt had taken a barge up the Missouri River along the 1840 route of the early fur traders. Drawing upon his impressions of the river and the historical documents, he wrote a 600-page epic poem called *A Cycle of the West*.

The university realized that Neihardt might not be around much longer, so before each class they wired him for sound. Cords ran from microphones clipped on his chest to tape recorders on the floor of the lecture hall. In spite of these distractions, when he read, the wires seemed to vanish along with the seats and even the stage. I felt like we were camped out in the Rocky Mountains, listening to an old fur trapper spin yarns about trapping beaver and fighting Indians in the wilderness. Neihardt's voice quivered and quaked as I listened in awe. I doubt that Homer could have given a finer performance reciting the tales of the Trojan Wars. One of my favorite parts went,

But when . . . we started for the sea
That summer, Bob, not one of seventeen,
I'll warrant, cared to know what life might mean.
To ask that question is a kind of dying.
What matters to a bird awing is flying;
What matters to a proper thirst is drinking.
A tree would wither if it got to thinking
Of what the summers and the winters meant.
There was a place to go and we went,
High-hearted with a hunger for the new.
The fifty mules and horses felt so too
For all their heavy packs. The brutes are wise
Beyond us, Bob. They can't philosophize
And get the world all tangled in their skulls.

After Neihardt read those words he looked up and said, "If you remember no other of my words, remember these. They'll help you live someday."

9
POPSICLE STICKS
Missouri – Summer 1975

SINCE MY DAYS at the University of Missouri I had tried not to philosophize, but lacking a philosophy to live by wasn't easy either. As we drove through the cold prairie night, I began to wonder what it would have been like if I hadn't flunked out of college. Would I have become a war correspondent? Would I be married with kids? Did I really want to be a journalist or a mountain man? I stopped myself and realized I'd fallen into the trap. I was getting the world all tangled up in my skull.

The next day, as we approached Columbia, Missouri, the air grew hot and sticky. The air conditioner wasn't working, so we began looking for a place to cool off. A clerk at a truck stop told us where we could find a popular swimming hole that had once been a rock quarry.

After driving around for a while, we ran into two couples who were looking for the same spot. We shared ideas and finally stumbled upon the abandoned quarry filled with clear spring water. Hundreds of people lined the banks. Some were clothed; some weren't. We went to the end of the quarry with the preponderance of nude bathers and stripped down. Everyone, that is, but Ken-Adi. Always the nonconformist, he donned a 1920's-style bathing suit and jumped in. One of the women, a nursing student, was very well-endowed. When we finished our swim, I sat next to her on a rock as we dried our bodies in the sun and talked. I tried to discuss her field of study, but all I could think about was nursing.

After we cooled off with some beer, one of the couples invited us to spend the night with them in Columbia where they had a small house with a large front porch. Another couple joined us. Behind the house was a well-tended garden with rows of sweet corn, melons, squash, cucumbers, carrots, radishes, tomatoes and herbs. Ken-Adi, who had grown up on small dairy farm near Madison, expertly selected the vegetables for our dinner. The six of us sat on cushions around a sheet of plywood covered with a white sheet resting on four hassocks.

Ken-Adi sat at the head of the table. Before him were earthenware dishes of fresh squash, sweet potatoes and green beans. The hostess, a short, stocky woman with long black braided hair, brought in a steaming tray stacked with sweet corn and placed it in the middle of the table. She served each of us a salad bowl piled high with greens, tomatoes and nuts. Before dinner, Ken-Adi asked everyone to bow their head for a prayer.

He began, "Thank you God for this bounty we are about to receive . . ." He paused, as if deciding what to say next. "And thank you for the good karma we are experiencing . . . and may your light shine on our lives . . . and protect us on our journey throughout life as we all search within ourselves for the cosmic whole of our existence on this plane . . . and . . . ah . . . amen."

We spent the night in a spare bedroom and left the next morning. I tried to locate the Lewis and Clark residence center where I had lived while I was at the university, but we got lost and ended up near the interstate. We left Columbia and drove west on I-70 through the broad rolling cornfields of Missouri until we hit Kansas City, then turned south on I-35 toward Wichita. Near the Flint Hills the landscape shifted to smaller sculpted hills of brilliant green with hues of yellow. The late afternoon sun highlighted the openness of the land as shadows deepened the curves and the colors became tinged with gold.

At about 4 P.M. we arrived in Wichita, a mid-sized prairie town, with wide, newly paved roads, trimmed lawns and well kept houses. We collected our deposit and turned the keys over to the owner who gave us a ride downtown.

Then, for the first time, we stood in the middle of the continent totally dependent on the good will of strangers. I looked around. Everybody looked plain — no long hair, no street musicians, no skateboards. This was no place for a guru in a white turban and his mustachioed sidekick toting backpacks. I felt self-conscious and eager to move on. But to Ken-Adi, who was completely oblivious to our new predicament, we might as well have been walking down State Street in Madison. I was glad we didn't have any dope. Although I frequently partook of the herb, I never saw Ken-Adi smoke even one joint. Somehow he managed to maintain a sunny, almost childlike disposition toward life, without using drugs, a quality that I greatly admired.

As we shuffled down the side of the road toward the interstate, Ken-Adi veered off and crossed the lawn of a Catholic church.

"Where are you going?" I called out, but by then he was already halfway across the lawn, heading for a side door.

"You wanna get us arrested for trespassing? You know, this isn't Madison."

"Don't worry, Richard. I'll just be a minute."

There was nothing left to do but follow him in.

The door to the pews was open and nobody was there, so Ken-Adi marched right down the center aisle and genuflected before a statue of the Virgin Mary. After a silent prayer he got up and we headed for the door.

"What did you pray for?"

"I prayed for my Guru, Yogi Bajan," he said.

"How about us?" I asked. "How about praying that we have a safe trip?"

"I feel the karma all around us Richard. It's good. Don't worry."

As we were leaving, a priest approached us.

Ken-Adi greeted him with a friendly, "Hello, you've got a beautiful church." The priest gave us the once over, smiled and continued walking down the hall. That was the first time I realized a church was open to anyone.

I decided that we would hitch north into Nebraska then catch I-80 west toward Wyoming. We left the church and tried to hitch a ride to the interstate, but people just slowed down and gawked at us. We walked several miles and finally came to I-135. Ken-Adi had never hitched the interstates, so it was up to me to get us a ride. I selected a spot on an entrance ramp to avoid being ticketed.

We hadn't been standing there long when a state trooper pulled up on the other side of the ramp and asked us for ID's. We crossed the road, gave him our driver's licenses then walked back to the other side while he checked us for outstanding warrants. Ken-Adi took a banana from his pack and began eating it. A couple minutes later we cleared the radio check and the trooper handed us back our licenses.

"In this state it constitutes a misdemeanor offense to be soliciting a ride on the interstate highway system," he said.

"Yes, sir. I realize that. That's why we're hitching on the entrance ramp," I replied, trying not to sound like a wise ass.

He looked up at me from his squad car.

Ken-Adi finished his banana, carefully folded the peel and put it in his pack.

"You know, I'm very careful about littering," he told the trooper.

The trooper nodded.

"I have great respect for this land," said, Ken-Adi. "I noticed there are all kinds of things along here that people threw out of their cars," he said. I wondered what he was getting at. The trooper nodded again, perhaps wondering the same thing.

"Is it against the law to throw candy wrappers on the ground?" Ken-Adi asked. He sounded almost childlike.

"Yes, it is."

Ken-Adi looked at the ground. "Is it against the law to throw popsicle sticks on the ground?"

"Yes, it is. There is a fine for littering."

"How about cigarette butts? There's a lot of cigarette butts on the ground," said Ken-Adi.

The trooper stared at him through his gold, wire-rimmed, state trooper sunglasses then shifted his stare to me. I looked away. Was Ken-Adi messing with his mind? He sounded so sincere with his white turban and gauze pants flapping in the prairie wind.

The trooper turned back to him and said, "Yes, cigarette butts are against the law, too."

Ken-Adi now became relentless, asking the trooper about bottle caps, paper cups, napkins, plastic forks, straws, and pop bottles. I walked to the front of the car and turned my head away to laugh. When I turned back, the trooper, who had remained in his car the entire time, was revving his engine.

"You boys just stay off the interstate."

We backed away. "OK, no problem. Thanks," I said. Ken-Adi waved good-bye as the trooper peeled out and rapidly accelerated up the entrance ramp.

Unfortunately this would not be our only brush with the law.

10
DOBERMANS IN OUTER SPACE
Nebraska to Utah – Summer 1975

AROUND SUNSET we got a ride north to a large truck stop near North Platt, Nebraska. It was a massive encampment of restaurants, gas pumps, truck washes, acres of parking lots and diesel rigs silhouetted against the orange and red sky.

We walked half-way through a curve on an entrance ramp to Interstate-80 and waited for another ride. I played *Oh Susanna* on my harmonica and Ken-Adi did a little dance to keep warm. Suddenly two blinding headlights came around the curve. I shielded my eyes. Instead of turning, the driver came over the lip of grass in front of us and stopped. The vehicle looked like a pick-up truck because its lights were high off the ground. I stopped playing my harmonica. A wave of fear spread over me. This was redneck cowboy country.

An amplified voice came from behind the lights.

"Turn around and put your hands on the railing. Spread your legs." We assumed the position.

I heard two truck doors slam and the sound of gravel crunching as two men approached.

The cowboys patted us down. One wore a silver badge. I relaxed a little. At least we weren't being robbed.

"How about some ID's, fellas," said the stocky one with the badge. I turned around, removed my driver's license from my wallet and handed it to him.

"They just checked us in Kansas," I said.

"This is Nebraska, son," he said and walked back to his truck.

I hoped Ken-Adi would keep quiet this time.

"How long you boys been out here?" asked the other deputy, sounding a little friendlier.

"We just got here," said Ken-Adi, bouncing up and down on his toes, trying to keep warm.

The deputy was silhouetted against the headlights and I had to squint to see him. His breath made white trails of steam in the cool damp air. I imagined he was looking us over or wondering whether he should search our packs.

"Where you boys headed?"

I answered quickly before Ken-Adi had a chance. "We're going to California. Gonna visit some friends."

"Oh, well, you'll get a ride," he said appearing satisfied with my answer. "They all get out. Sometimes we've got 15 or 20 lined up here. We arrested one here last week, escaped from the state mental hospital," he said, smiling proudly like he had just bagged an antelope.

The other deputy returned and handed us our licenses. "You boys just stay off the highway and you'll be all right," he said. They got back in their truck and left.

We finally got a ride out of North Platt with a guy from New York who needed help driving. We dozed a little in shifts. The stars grew dimmer and the black silhouettes of the mountains became sharper as dawn broke on a cloudless sky. About mid-morning we rolled through the outskirts of Cheyenne, Wyoming, the place where the real west began for me. West of Cheyenne the road opened up onto barren hills and clumps of sagebrush extending to the horizon. The air grew dry and smelled sweetly of sage and dust.

We traveled all day and made it to Rock Springs that evening. Rock Springs was actually two towns, one enclosing the other. The center was the remnant of a small, run-down desert oasis with a dilapidated stone hotel, a feed store, and a couple of small bars. Encircling the old town were thousands of trailers, brought in by construction workers who worked at the hydroelectric power plants along the Green River. Bulldozers and earth scrapers were parked in vacant lots and alongside roads. Piles of broken concrete lay next to long rows of string indicating where new sidewalks would be built.

The town was located in a desolate area of sun-scorched rocks and dirt, as if God had plopped it down in the middle of nowhere and dared it to survive. Cowboys and roughnecks drove their old cars and pick-up trucks down the rugged streets after work leaving long trails of dust and looking for places to get drunk.

We checked into the hotel downtown. That night we dined at a little Mexican café. As we walked in, Ken-Adi stopped, sniffed the air and looked around the room, fixing his stare on a slim, dark-haired waitress wearing black jeans and a colorfully embroidered Mexican blouse. We sat down at a booth in the corner.

"You know Richard, there's a lot of strong karma here. I've just got to make contact with it," Ken-Adi said. He took a deep breath, put his elbows on the table and brought his outstretched fingers together in front of him, as if he was trying to trap some stray cosmic energy.

The waitress walked slowly across the room as we were talking and placed menus on our table.

"How are you this evening?" she asked.

Ken-Adi looked up with wide eyes and stared at her for a couple seconds before answering. "We're just fine. You know, you've got beautiful eyes."

She immediately broke eye contact and said curtly, "I'll be back when you decide what you want."

As she left the room I leaned over and whispered, "She's probably been hustled by hundreds of roughnecks and saddle tramps. Maybe she's married. One thing's for sure, she doesn't want much to do with us."

"Didn't you feel the karma?" Ken-Adi asked.

"Yeah, it was bad karma," I replied. We were in a strange town and I didn't want to take any chances hassling the locals.

"We made contact there for a second," he went on. "I felt something."

"She's got pretty eyes, okay?" I replied.

When she came back, Ken-Adi asked her if they had any tofu.

"What?" she asked.

"Tofu, it's made from bean curds," he explained. "I try and stay away from meat. It's very impure. I find that it blocks the natural flow of love in the universe."

She stared at Ken-Adi for a few seconds. No, she wasn't going to encourage him. "We've got tacos with beans," she said, "but none of that other stuff." We both ordered Mexican omelets.

After we had eaten, Ken-Adi wrote her a note on a napkin. He wrote that he felt a cosmic love for her, then apologized for making her uncomfortable. If she would like to discuss things further, the note went on, he could meet her after work. He drew a yin-yang symbol on the napkin and handed it to her when she brought our checks. She dropped the napkin back on the table and walked away.

In the morning we waited for a ride on an entrance ramp without much luck. I decided to take a chance and moved up the ramp to the interstate. We waited several hours along a high, barren, desert plateau. The view was stark and Precambrian, as if we had been transported back to when plants had not yet evolved.

Ken-Adi, moved by the vastness of the landscape, unrolled his sheepskin and assumed the full lotus position, tucking each foot into the fold behind his knees, spreading his arms to the side and delicately making a circle with his thumb and index finger. Once in position, he closed his eyes and smiled. Cars whizzed by. I faced the road with my thumb out and tried not to look at him. After a few minutes he went from a full lotus into a headstand, using his elbows to prop himself up. I'd had enough. Serious hitchhiker etiquette had been breached

"Jesus," I shouted, "How the hell are we gonna get a ride with you standing on your head? I wanta get out of here sometime today."

Ken-Adi sat up and put away his sheepskin. The desert wind increased as the sun got lower in the sky and whipped up the fine sand into miniature vortexes that danced across the ground.

"I was just praying for a ride," he said.

"Well, your karma must be a little off today," I said, "because we've been out here for five hours."

I was about to head back into town for some water and a break from Ken-Adi when a pick-up truck stopped for us. We ran around back to throw our packs in but stopped abruptly when a Doberman Pinscher raised its head and growled. The driver was a tall, muscular man with sunglasses and a cowboy hat. He got out of the truck, walked to the back, and began scratching the dog behind its ears.

"He won't hurt you, his bark is worse than his bite," he said as the dog put its head down and continued a low growl.

I looked at Ken-Adi, who smiled, walked confidently up to the dog and began rubbing its head.

"Glad to see you've made a friend," I said. "You can ride with him." I threw my pack in the back, climbed into the front seat and we were off. After a couple minutes I turned around and Ken-Adi was huddled in the corner, the dog's head in his lap.

The driver, a civilian technician for the Air Force, had recently finished calibrating some sensitive equipment at Cheyenne Mountain, Colorado, headquarters of the North American Aerospace Defense Command (NORAD) and the nerve center for America's nuclear defense systems. However, that didn't keep him from offering me a toke from his hash pipe. We got high.

As we drove I spaced out on the desert and remembered my last experience with nuclear weapons in the Navy back in 1969. I had just finished two deployments to Vietnam with the Seabees and was assigned to the USS Orion, a submarine tender. The Orion was a big, World War II vintage ship, docked most of the time in Norfolk, Virginia. We repaired and resupplied nuclear attack submarines as they came off patrol.

I had a friend named Ken who was a Boatswains Mate. Bozuns, as they were called, were in charge of the routine operations of the ship like maintenance and security. Ken and I would often leave the ship during lunch hour, drive around and get high. After we got back one day, I was watching a working party transfer a nuclear missile from the Orion to a submarine. The missile was suspended from a crane and Ken, standing there with his full beard and mirror sunglasses, was guiding it into a tube protruding from the main deck of the sub. As the missile was lowered to within Ken's grasp, he spun it so the tail fins could be inserted first. I hoped he wasn't as stoned as I was. Once properly positioned, the missile was slowly slipped down the tube.

I remembered an earlier incident where the entire crew of a sub was thrown in the brig after a pot-dealing ring was uncovered and a skeleton crew manned the sub while it was in port. Is this how it was all going to end, I wondered? Were we going to destroy civilization because some stoned technician made an awful mistake? The more powerful weapons we had, the less security they provided.

We drove all night across high mountain prairies, the black sky choked with stars. With billions of suns out there, millions of planets must be capable of producing life. Of those millions of planets there were probably thousands with civilizations. On at least one of those planets I figured there must be a guy riding in a pick-up truck across a mountain range who just decided that there was some other guy on another planet in a pick-up truck looking in his direction.

We drove all night. The next morning we came down from the Wasatch Mountains into the hot, dry valley of the Great Salt Lake. Ken-Adi and I switched places when we stopped at a little Mexican fruit stand for something to drink. When I got in the back of the truck the dog was sleeping, but after we began moving it woke up, growled and bared its teeth.

"Hey big fellow, take it easy," I said using a soothing tone. "I wouldn't want you to get lonely back here."

I reached out to pet the dog on the head, but it only snapped at me. Better be careful, I thought. One rip at my jugular vein with those razor sharp teeth and what was left of me would be food for the buzzards. I wondered what I was doing wrong. How had Ken-Adi managed to tame this savage beast? The truck started to move, so I decided to make the best of it.

"OK, have it your way," I said, retreating into a corner. I covered my body with a tarp. Whenever I tried to change positions the dog began a low, rumbling growl that kept me in my place. I wondered if there were Dobermans in outer space.

11

A PARTING OF THE WAYS
Berkeley – Summer 1975

WE DROVE ALL DAY across the hot desert, and all night over the frigid Sierra Nevada Mountains. The next morning we arrived in Davis, California where we got out. Ken-Adi kissed the Doberman good-bye.

I was tired, sore, cold and in a foul mood.

"How the hell can you kiss that son-of-a-bitch when he tried to rip my head off!" I yelled.

Ken-Adi gave me a startled look. "You should try putting out a little more cosmic love, Richard. I think he sensed your hostility as soon as you got in the back."

Fuck cosmic love. By now I had decided that Ken-Adi may be a step along the road to enlightenment, but he certainly wasn't my guru. I had to break free. I figured that he should have picked up enough hitchhiking smarts by watching me; if he hadn't it was time to learn.

"Look," I said. "Berkeley is a straight shot from here. I think it'll be easier if we hitch separately then meet at the ashram." I lied about meeting him at the ashram. I wanted to strike out on my own. "I'll give you first try," I said pointing to the entrance ramp.

"But Richard, we made it all the way here together. I don't think we'll have any trouble getting out of here."

"Yes, yes, we will," I said, trying not to sound desperate as I groped for an idea. "These people are city drivers. They're more distrustful than the cross-country drivers who are closer to the land . . . more into their money and cars and materialistic lifestyle. We'll get out a lot quicker this way, you'll see."

He turned around and looked at the entrance ramp. A steady stream of cars was heading west.

"All right, Richard," he said hesitantly. Ken-Adi crossed to the right side of the ramp, placed his pack on the shoulder of the road and stood there with his thumb out. He looked lost and I felt a twinge of guilt, like a father kicking out his young son. How would he deal with the cops and the drunks and the perverts that cruise the highways? When the traffic thinned he took a Frisbee from his pack, threw it to me and waved.

I threw it back to him. "You better put that away or we'll never get out of here," I shouted, trying not to cave in.

He threw it back to me again. What if I kept it? What if he came over and got it? I couldn't risk that. Then I'd have to talk him back to the other side. I threw him the Frisbee.

"I don't want the fucking Frisbee," I yelled. "Stick out your thumb."

As he put his thumb out, a car pulled over and he got in. I waved good-bye and he waved back. I watched him disappear into the morning rush hour traffic and relaxed. A new phase of the trip was beginning. I crossed to the other side of the ramp and stuck out my thumb.

I got a ride with a young student and ended up in Berkeley on Telegraph Avenue, a long crowded street filled with street vendors near the University of California campus. As I rested on a cement bench I looked around. Most of the people there were young with long hair, dressed in jeans and sneakers. However, one young woman stood out from the crowd. She was beautiful with long, honey- blond hair and a wholesome Midwestern look. She was handing out leaflets in a cocktail dress with stockings and high heels. A cocktail dress? On Telegraph Avenue? I decided to check this out and walked over to her. She smiled. "Hello," she said, looking me straight in the eye. "Would you like to come to dinner with me?"

Whoa! Was this really happening? I'm in Berkeley for five minutes and a beautiful blonde asks me out. I smiled at her and she smiled back.

Then she handed me one of the leaflets.

"Have you ever heard of the Reverend Sun-Myung Moon?" she asked.

My smile faded. I'd heard of Sun-Myung Moon, the right-wing Korean minister whose followers were the blissed-out Moonies. But this woman didn't have zombie eyes and a fake smile. She appeared very normal.

"Yeah, so? Where do you want to go for lunch?" I asked glancing at the leaflet.

She just smiled.

I stood there smiling back at her feeling a little awkward. "So what does your church believe in?" I asked.

"We believe in love and togetherness," she said.

Was this a come on? "Sounds great to me," I said. "That's it? Love and togetherness?" I was skeptical.

"If you want to know more we're having a feast at the church this evening," she said, brushing a wisp of hair from her eyes. "When you decide to join, the doctrines of our father will be revealed to you." She turned to a bearded young man who had been eavesdropping on our conversation. "Hello," she said to him. "Would you like to have dinner with me tonight?

What a let down, I thought. No date.

I wasn't going to join, but I was low on money and I needed a hot meal. I kept the leaflet and spent the rest of the afternoon hanging out.

At five-o-clock I went to the church. As I entered the vestibule, three short-haired young men reminiscent of the 1950's, dressed in suits, were playing Peter, Paul and Mary folk songs on their guitars. The corners of their lips were twisted into fake smiles as they rushed mechanically through their songs. It seemed incongruous. Why were these geeks trying to get converts in an area with such a strong counterculture? Maybe they were mining the same vein of lost souls that Charlie Manson had when recruiting for his murderous "family."

I walked past the musicians into a large room where dozens of people were kneeling at a low table covered with large bowls of rice and vegetarian gruel. Not much of a meal. The blond was nowhere in sight, so I took a plate and loaded up. I slammed the food down as quickly as possible and left. Later I located a youth hostel where I spent the night. I dreamed of Asian women with blond hair trying to seduce me with turnips and chocolate truffles.

12
FREEWAY ECOSYSTEM
Los Angeles – Summer 1975

THE NEXT DAY was misty and cool, so I climbed inside a Goodwill box and scrounged a sweater. I left Berkeley and hitched south toward Los Angeles where my friend Dan Kelly lived. We had taken journalism courses together at Columbia College in Chicago where I went after I got out of the Navy.

The college was a small urban school located downtown and offered a BA in Journalism without the hassle of a foreign language requirement. I used my veteran's benefits for living expenses and borrowed the money for tuition. I started classes in the fall of 1970.

The central part of the college consisted of three floors of an office building and was located five blocks north of the Loop. Some departments, such as film and dance, were spread throughout the city in rented spaces.

I met Kelly in one of my writing classes. He was a tall, gangly guy with over-the-ears, early-Beatles style hair and thick, square, wire-rimmed glasses. Kelly had a great sense of humor and helped me get through many tough times with Linda. He was a native Chicagoan and lived with his parents and grandparents in the working class suburb of Austin. His father was a janitorial supervisor at a high school and his grandfather, who lived upstairs with his grandmother, ran a men's clothing store. I sometimes envied the support and stability his family provided.

I arrived in the "City of the Angels" late that night and called Kelly from the interstate. He picked me up and took me to Costa Mesa where he shared an apartment with his girlfriend. It was located on the second floor of a small complex with a nicely landscaped courtyard.

Kelly had dropped out of law school and was selling iron-on decals for Betty Boop tee-shirts to head shops and souvenir stores. The next day we drove around town in his Mustang convertible making deliveries

The size and beauty of the freeways was incredible. These weren't just roads. These were miles of manufactured ecosystems inserted into traffic islands, The Desert Freeway Ecosystem. There were palm trees, cacti and succulents of all kinds scattered amidst the soil and rocks. Lizards, beetles and small mice were prey for birds and automobile tires. The freeway was an exotic way-station for species hitchhiking on tire treads and truck beds that could exist in a high carbon monoxide environment with frequent disruptions of their life cycles, not unlike the two-legged architects of their world.

Everyone was in a hurry, racing, passing, weaving in and out and riding each other's bumpers. After a couple hours of driving around I turned to Kelly.

"How do you handle all this?" I shouted through the loud music blaring from his stereo.

"Handle what?" he said.

"All this." I extended my arms in the air. "This. This, this . . . madness."

"Well, it's like this. When I lived in Chicago I used to get up in the morning, take a shower, have breakfast and go to work. Now I do almost the same thing. I get up in the morning, have a joint, take a shower and go to work, speaking of which . . ." he took a joint from the glove compartment, ". . . would you like to partake of one?"

Apparently this desert highway ecosystem created conditions in which adaptation required the inhaling of psychotropic herbs. I lit the joint, took a long draw and handed it to Kelly. I lay my head back on the seat and let the sun bake my face as Mariachi music played on the radio. Suddenly Kelly jerked the car onto an exit and pulled into a hot dog stand.

"Hey man," I protested. "I can't eat that junk food. I'm tryin' to clean out my body."

"High energy food, that's what you need," taunted Kelly. He ordered two foot-long hot dogs with the works, two Cokes and two hot fudge sundaes for both of us. I was in the grip of an evil salesman, determined to break down my newly acquired dietary taboos. What's worse, I was very hungry.

After we got the food Kelly pulled back on the freeway. He shoved the hot dog into his mouth with one hand and steered with the other. He had the Coke between his legs and the sundae sat precariously on his lap. We woofed down our food with abandon.

From Costa Mesa we turned west, toward Balboa Beach, where we stopped and took a walk on the pier. A cool late afternoon breeze was blowing in from the sea. A young woman in a bikini was walking through the gentle waves. She moved gracefully through the surf like a young doe prancing through a clear mountain stream, pausing occasionally to sniff the air.

After sunset we drove back to Kelly's apartment where we had dinner and swapped stories about Columbia College late into the night.

I was tired of the road and looked forward to hanging out for a couple days to recharge my batteries. Kelly had other ideas.

13
SAN FELIPE
Summer 1975

WHEN THE WEEKEND ARRIVED Kelly suggested we drive down to Mexico for a few days. He knew a secluded little fishing village called San Felipe on the East Coast of Baja California, right below Mexicali. Although I was tired, I'd never been to Mexico, so the idea sounded exciting.

We piled some clothes and suntan lotion into his Mustang and took off. We reached Calexico by noon and bought a weekend's worth of Mexican liability insurance from a vending machine then crossed the border into Mexacali and headed into the desert.

The road was severely buckled from the heat, with potholes and patches everywhere. Occasionally we'd pass shacks thrown together with scrap tin and lumber, some with chicken coops attached. There were no trees, only baked ground and rugged brown hills. I wondered how the people who lived there survived. They were eking out a living in this godforsaken land while I was on vacation from LA. I began to feel a little guilty. Perhaps in my next life I'd come back as a desert lizard.

About 2 P.M., as we neared San Felipe, I began looking for signs of shade trees planted by settlers around the town, like on the Great Plains. I saw nothing but desert.

"It's just up ahead a couple of miles," Kelly said, anticipating my question.

"I sure could use a cold beer and a swimming pool," I shot back.

As we rounded a curve there it was — a small town, next to the ocean, barren of vegetation and clogged with thousands of cars and dirt bikes.

"What the hell is going on?" I yelled to Kelly. "I thought this was a quiet little fishing village."

"Well, that's what my neighbor said."

We looked for a motel, but all the rooms were taken.

After deciding to make the best of it we stopped for a beer at a local cantina. Inside a Mariachi band played and a crowd cheered as a Mexican cowboy, wearing a fancy black sombrero and black clothes embroidered with silver spangles, stomped his heels on the wood floor and jumped back and forth through a lariat. After the performance we downed our beers and bought a case of Coronas for six bucks. We decided to head back to LA. When we got to the border a guard checked our entry ticket and waved us to the side.

"What's going on, Kelly?" I asked.

"I don't know," he answered, "This has never happened to me before."

A couple of armed U.S. Border Patrolmen asked us if we had anything to declare.

"Just this case of beer," said Kelly, pointing to the Coronas in the back seat.

They surveyed rear seat, then stepped back and scrutinized the car.

"Could you open your trunk, sir?" asked one of the officers. Kelly obliged.

The guard motioned to me. "Please get out and both of you put your hands on the side of the car and spread your legs," he said.

We did as he requested. Why didn't they believe us? Then it hit me. They probably wondered why two guys would go all the way to San Felipe and come back a few hours later with only a case of beer. I hoped Kelly hadn't left any roaches in the cracks of his car seat.

They patted us down.

"Take your right hand, reach into your pocket and take out your wallet," a big cop with a bushy mustache asked.

I leaned against the wall with my left hand and gave him my wallet.

He studied our driver's licenses for a long time.

"So Mr. Chamberlin, you came all the way from Wisconsin and only stayed in Mexico for less than a day?"

I stopped leaning against the wall. "Too many people down there," I replied. "We were looking for a relaxing vacation."

He looked up at us, then down at our licenses and then up at us again.

Was there a smuggling ring from Wisconsin operating south of the border?

"All right gentlemen," he said handing our wallets back.

He looked in the car one more time.

"You're gonna have to dump most of that beer. You're only allowed three bottles each."

We popped open the tops and poured the beer down a drain; relieved we weren't going to spend the night in jail.

PART THREE

VIETNAM

14

DEXTER'S DRONES

Great Lakes Naval Training Command – 1966

AS KELLY AND I DROVE NORTH, back to Los Angeles, we passed a Marine Corps bus full of recruits heading for boot camp at Camp Pendleton. It reminded me of a trip I had taken ten years earlier, to the Great Lakes Naval Training Center north of Chicago.

I had flunked out of the University of Missouri in June of 1966. That summer when I contacted my draft board in Miami they gave me two choices — volunteer or get drafted. Until that Spring, I had never seriously considered joining the military. There was no military tradition in our family, and I never thought I had an obligation to serve. My father avoided serving in World War II because of a knee injury, but decided to join the Merchant Marine. He went to Sheepshead Bay in New York for training, but went AWOL after he realized German subs were sinking supply convoys in the North Atlantic. He returned to Madison, where he and my mother taught Morse code to GI's.

Although I didn't want to join the military, I still thought of myself as a patriotic American. I viewed the emerging war protests as the actions of a small minority of malcontents and radicals. I believed President Johnson when he said America must help protect a small, defenseless South Vietnam from communist aggression. However, I had no illusions about the war being a heroic endeavor. Although the only experience I'd had with war was in the movie theater, I was pretty sure real war was much different. The good guys died, sometimes by the horrible mistakes of their own officers. Many soldiers returned as amputees or were horribly disfigured. If I had to go, I wouldn't resist. I just wanted to come home in one piece.

I could have joined the Army for two years, but I wanted to avoid slogging through swamps and getting shot at. The Navy required four years of active duty, but they guaranteed me a special school and a higher pay grade because I'd had some college.

I took the swearing-in ceremony in a large room on a hot day in downtown Miami with about twenty other young men. We all raised our right hands and repeated the oath in unison.

"I swear to uphold the Constitution of the United States and to defend it against all enemies both foreign and domestic. . . ."

At the end of the ceremony, the young Hispanic sergeant who administered the oath said, "You are now members of the military forces of the United States. Be proud of that." Then, looking at the motley assemblage of young men, he gave us a disdainful look and added, "Be proud of something for the first time in your lives."

I was proud and left with my shoulders back and my head held high. I was now a man who would be called upon to defend his country. After being rejected for so long by academia and living with the fear of being drafted, I was immensely grateful.

Since I was on a delayed entry plan I didn't have to go on active duty until the fall. That summer our family moved to Kentucky where my dad got a job selling land. I got a temporary job in Louisville doing inventory at a chemical warehouse.

On the afternoon of September 5, 1966, I boarded a commercial flight to Chicago with a group of other enlistees. After we landed at Chicago's O'Hare Airport, we took buses to the Great Lakes Naval Recruit Training Center north of the city.

It was dark when we got there. We pulled up to a guard shack next to a wire fence, and a Marine waved us through. We stopped near a row of red brick barracks and filed off the bus. There were no drill sergeants bellowing orders at us like I had seen in the movies; only two sleepy recruits, their pant legs tucked into white canvas spats which were laced over their boots like a revolutionary war soldier. They escorted us to the barracks where we spent the night.

I didn't sleep well. There was a rumor going around about getting a shot in the left testicle with a square needle. Not likely, I reasoned. Square needles don't exist, but round needles do. Why would they give us shots there anyway, I thought? It was probably just an exaggeration. But what if it was true? I had just signed away my freedom. Could they force me to get a shot in the testicle? Before I left Louisville I was a free man, but now I felt extremely vulnerable, lying in a fetal position on a lumpy mattress in a stuffy, crowded dormitory with a bunch of strangers.

In the morning we stowed our civilian clothes and were issued blue dungaree fatigues. Next we had our heads shaved. Hippies, bikers, and cowboys went in one side of the barbershop and bald-headed clones emerged from the other. When I looked in a mirror I barely recognized myself. In the days that followed we became a recruit company of eighty men and were given a number — 546. Soon we learned to recognize each other by our faces and regional accents, not by the way we dressed or the length of our hair.

After a week of being marched around in a constant state of fatigue and confusion, I'd had enough. I thought I was special. I had three years of college. I deserved to be treated with respect. I wanted to be an officer. However, I was disappointed when I discovered Officer's Candidate School was only taking college graduates. Two-thirds of the company had some college and most had enlisted for the same reason I did — to avoid the draft.

Eventually we got shuttled from the processing center to the main training base, an area of modern three-story barracks adjacent to spacious asphalt drill areas called grinders. Our company commander was a First Class Boatswain's Mate named Dexter who was absent during most of our training. When he did show up he was frequently drunk. His assistant was a kid named Shiniman who was still only a seaman. We had to refer to him as "Mister Shiniman." He showed us how to shine our boots, fold our laundry and make our beds. In a week I had gone from the exhilaration of hoping to become an officer to the humiliation of calling a kid two years younger than me "Mister."

I can't remember how the recruit command was chosen, but an ex-construction foreman from Indiana named Jack became our Recruit Petty Officer in Charge (RPOC). Jack was a short, stocky man with thick biceps who appointed a big baby-faced southern cracker as his Recruit Master-At-Arms, second in command. Jack also hand picked his platoon leaders.

When we weren't in class we spent hours on the grinder trying to perfect our marching skills. Once, after an especially humiliating drill, Jack took all the platoon leaders into the shower room and intimidated them, slamming them against the wall and cussing them out. This did little to improve our marching skills.

One day, as we were marching in formation, Jack yelled out, "You know what a drone is? A drone is a male bee and all he does is lay around and fuck the queen. That's what you guys are. You want to lie around all day and fuck off. You're Dexter's Drones." The name stuck.

Day after day we endured hours of marching, harassment and sleep deprivation. The physical punishment and the emotional stress became so intense I wanted to quit, but something inside wouldn't let me. Besides, I had signed up for four years active duty and in a time of war the government took that contract very seriously. To drive home the point, the Navy had devised a series of punishments for reluctant recruits.

One punishment was called Happy Hour, rigidly supervised calisthenics. I forgot to strip the sheets from my bed one day and was given two Happy Hours to work off back-to-back.

At the appointed hour I ran (recruits weren't allowed to walk) to the drill hall, a huge Quonset building that was slightly smaller than a football field. I entered and took my place in line with a group of about two hundred other recruits who had screwed up. A drill instructor and several recruit helpers were on a stage in front of us.

The drill instructor announced to us that we were there because we lacked military discipline. He said self-discipline is preferable to military discipline, but that in the absence of self-discipline, military discipline would have to do.

After the speech, the exercises commenced. We did push-ups, jumping jacks, leg lifts, and sit-ups. Every exercise had to be performed in unison and just one person out of cadence would cause the whole group to repeat it. After a hundred jumping jacks, which we all counted out loudly, in unison, everyone was supposed to bring their legs together and their arms down to their sides without slapping their thighs. Invariably someone would slap their thighs and we'd have to repeat the whole thing.

While doing the push-ups we'd all have to spell out M-I-L-I-T-A-R-Y D-I-S-C-I-P-L-I-N-E, one letter at a time in unison each time we pushed up.

"What do you lack?" bellowed the drill instructor.

"Military discipline," came the earnest reply from two hundred aching recruits, but we didn't say, "Sir," so we had to spell the words again.

"On your bellies, begin," the drill instructor ordered.

We pushed up. "M!" we shouted. We lowered ourselves to the deck, bounced back up and shouted "I!" The drill hall echoed with two hundred "I's."

When we finished spelling both words, he asked again, "Now, what do you lack?" The reply, "Military discipline, Sir," reverberated throughout the hall.

"And what is the best form of discipline?" he taunted. "Self-discipline, Sir," we cried out, still in the "up" position from the last count of "E."

"All right now," our tormentor said, lowering his voice. For the first time he actually sounded friendly. "Are you getting tired?"

No one dared answer because it sounded like a trick question.

"Well, if you aren't tired you can stay there all day," he said as our muscles began to quiver and some bellies sagged toward the deck.

After a couple minutes, he said, "Do you want to rest?"

The request sounded like another trick question, but several recruits cried out, "Yes, sir."

"What did you say? I can't hear you," he said in a mocking tone.

Suddenly everyone was yelling, "Yes sir. Yes sir, Yes sir." Quickly we began to shout it in unison. "YES SIR."

"Okay, everyone, over on your backs," he commanded.

As soon as we had dropped to the deck and rolled over, he yelled, "Everyone, get those boots off my deck." Soon everyone was grunting again, trying to keep their boots from touching the floor.

After several minutes he said, "Well, has everyone had enough rest?" Everyone said they had and we were called to attention.

He gave us another lecture, this time about how easy we had it compared to the Marines and how sloppy civilians were. After another hour of more calisthenics, some recruits started throwing up and the recruit assistants gave them buckets to fill. Other recruits were rolling on the floor with muscle cramps. When we were through, I limped back to the barracks, a wounded drone. It took several days for the knots to leave my muscles.

Happy Hour was just the first phase of the punishment gauntlet. Next came the Mouse House, a special barracks where all recruits did was wash clothes, dry clothes, fold clothes then wash the same clothes again repeating the process over and over until they learned how to fold clothes or went crazy. The last punishment was the brig, a compound circled with barbed wire guarded by Marines. There we were told, the Marines "beat the shit out of candy-assed sailors and enjoyed it." Only after spending time in the brig did the Navy grant a "Failure To Adapt To Military Life" discharge. I never made it to the Mouse House or beyond. I began to use self-discipline to keep my mind from drifting.

Eventually I graduated with Recruit Company 546 and tried to put the nonsensical arbitrariness of boot camp behind me. Instead I found out that the military nonsense was just beginning.

15

THE SEABEES
Gulfport, Mississippi – March 1967

MY FIRST CHOICE of a Navy school after boot camp was the one for Journalist Mate. I got my last choice, Storekeeper. After two weeks of leave, I began ten weeks of training in supply procedures at Newport, Rhode Island. Much of the class time was spent looking up Federal Identification Numbers (FIN's) in huge volumes of catalogues and filling out order forms. I hated Storekeeper School and graduated at the bottom of my class, but I didn't really care.

From Rhode Island, I was assigned to a Seabee battalion in Gulfport, Mississippi, home of the Twentieth Naval Construction Regiment. Gulfport was a small port city on the Gulf of Mexico, about seventy miles east of New Orleans. The base was covered with wide expanses of treeless, greenish-brown lawns. Most of the buildings were two-and three-story barracks, chow halls and battalion headquarters. A row of warehouses was located next to a railroad track.

Every battalion had about eight hundred men and was composed of specialized companies. Each company dealt with specific areas of construction such as welding, electrical work, carpentry, plumbing, transportation, heavy equipment, and coordination. I was attached to the Headquarters Company of Mobile Construction Battalion-74. The battalion was recently recommissioned after being inactive for a long time after serving in the Pacific during World War II. We were scheduled to deploy to the Republic of Vietnam in five months.

Our job as storekeepers was to outfit the battalion with enough supplies to last for eight months while in country. We also had to complete a three-week combat training course which included qualifying with the M-16 rifle and familiarizing ourselves with the M-60 machine gun and .45 caliber pistol. I liked the M-16 because it was light and sleek-looking. It was also easy to take apart and had no kick when fired. The .45 handgun, in contrast, was more primitive looking, like a heavy metal pipe with a handle. Some of our training was done in Gulfport and some was done in cooperation with the Marines at Camp Lejeune, North Carolina.

For our graduation exercise at Camp Lejeune, the battalion marched several miles down a dirt road to a spot in a pine forest where we dug in. We were supposed to defend our positions against the "Viet Cong" who were actually Marines just back from Vietnam.

We marched with rifles and full field packs along a dirt road repelling ambush rights and ambush lefts. The Marines used the older M-14 rifles, which were equipped with blank firing adapters (BFA's), so their shots sounded real. We used our M-16's with no BFA's and shouted "BANG" when we shot at the Marines.

When we arrived at our defensive position, we were forced to dig our foxholes while lying on our sides to keep from being "shot." The Marines sniped at us and we "shot" back.

After several hours the Marines stopped playing dead and then so did we. The officers called a time-out and met to decide who would be dead, under what conditions, and for how long. Still, the arguments continued. Cries of, "Bang, bang, you're dead." "No I'm not, you are," went on all day and it became quite embarrassing.

That night we crouched in our foxholes and waited for the Marines to attack. Instead of a frontal assault with BAF's blazing and smoke grenades going off, they snuck up behind us, tapped us on the shoulder and said, "You're dead, motherfucker." They wiped out the whole battalion that night.

The second night was even stranger. The air was cool and soggy as we shivered in our foxholes trying to stay awake. At about midnight, the "enemy" used a microphone and began bombarding us with inducements to surrender.

"Are you getting sleepy, Seabee?" they taunted. "Come on over to our side and rest. We have nice warm food and hot coffee for you."

We sent up an illumination flare. Our position and the bushes beyond the perimeter took on a reddish, surrealistic glow as the flare, which was suspended from a small parachute, drifted slowly downward, swaying slightly in the breeze and trailing white smoke until it landed somewhere in enemy territory.

"Why do you keep killing our people?" they called out. "Go home to your own country. Leave us alone. We only want peace."

This continued throughout the night. In my sleep-deprived brain, it seemed like we actually were in 'Nam. A few Seabees surrendered and invited us to join them. Meanwhile the Marines snuck around behind the lines tapping Seabees on the shoulder.

"Hey, asshole, you're dead."

16
MARY'S BAR
Gulfport – May 1967

AFTER WE RETURNED to Gulfport from Camp Lejeune, we had a month to prepare for our deployment to Vietnam. I was on the advanced party, so would spend an extra month in Vietnam before the rest of the battalion got there. We ordered supplies, packed crates, and shipped materials. In our off hours we cruised the bars, played pool, and took leaves to see our families.

My last night in town, I'd planned on blowing my money on booze and broads at the strip, a mile of sleazy bars and second-rate hotels between Biloxi and Gulfport. However, I never made it.

That morning I had begun to experience a strange detachment from my surroundings, like the emotional part of me had already left for 'Nam. I think it left in the middle of the five-day forecast on the radio.

"High today near 90," the weatherman said. "Low tonight 73 and sunny and hot again tomorrow. The five-day forecast is rain and drizzle later in the. . . ."

Why should I care? Rain, sun or snow, I'd be gone. Half of me was here, the other half was there. I felt alienated from everything around me and wondered if anyone else was feeling that way.

As I stepped outside the chow hall that morning, the bright southern sunlight hit me like a flash bulb. I put on my sunglasses and headed across the parched, brown lawn toward the three-storied white barracks.

The barracks was a long room with a high ceiling. Living pods of four lockers and bunks were arranged along each side of the room with a wide hall down the middle. Above the lockers, windows were open wide for cross-ventilation. Everyone was sleeping late on a Saturday morning. I walked down the aisles looking for someone to talk with. The only sounds were the humming of a ceiling fan and the snoring of men sprawled on their bunks in olive drab skivey shorts.

Later that night, I got together for drinks with a few friends from Headquarters Company at Mary's, a small bar just outside the main gate. The entrance to Mary's was a rusty screen door with dirty finger marks around the handle. The floor was cement. On the ceiling, four partially lit neon lights competed for space with two rotary fans, only one of which was lethargically cutting through the thick, warm air of the Gulf Coast. The fan did little to cool the room. Cigarette butts, wet napkins and empty beer cans littered our table.

I was there with two other storekeepers; Gary Howard, from a small town in Kentucky and Henry Goerke (the Gerk), from Long Island. The Gerk had worked at a Manhattan ad agency before he got his draft notice and joined the Navy to stay out of the Army. His face was pockmarked from acne, and he had a receding hairline. He was scornful of the military, the Seabees, the South and Southerners. Gary Howard was a quiet young man with black-framed glasses and a soft Kentucky accent.

The two of them were embroiled in an argument over the pronunciation of the word "egotistical."

"How many times do I have to tell you it's "ego-tist-ical," said the Gerk.

"Ah graduated from hah school, too," protested Gary. "Ah know how to spell and it's, ego-cis-tical, E-G-O-C-I-S-T-I-C-A-L."

"But that's not what the dictionary says. I showed it to you today, remember? We went to the fucking base library and looked it up."

"That was a northern dictionary," said Gary.

"What do you mean 'a northern dictionary'? They're all the same. Jesus Christ. A northern dictionary. Now I've heard it all," the Gerk said, throwing his hands in the air.

Gary just stared at his beer. The Gerk got up and went to the john. The fourth member of our little get-together was a civilian named Stew who had wandered into the bar and was buying us drinks.

Stew thought this was all great fun. He ate it up because he was a civilian and he didn't have to go to Vietnam, yet he wanted to be a part of us. Maybe he was living a fantasy about being with brave men going to war.

Stew had an annoying habit of striking a match to light his cigarette, letting the flame burn down, and then shaking it out just before it burned his finger tips. He had a wart on his chin that just hung there by a thread of tissue. I wished he would burn it off with the match. His flaccid, sagging face mirrored a monotonous life. This was a moment of stolen glory for him.

The warm beer at Mary's Bar was tasteless, so I poured mine down like water and hoped the alcohol would bring my mind back in line with my body. I didn't realize how drunk I was until I got up to make a phone call.

I staggered toward the door, but miscalculated and caught my right shoulder on the jamb. I ricocheted off and tried again. My pocket was full of change to call my girlfriend. I wasn't sure what I was supposed to do my last night in town so I was making it up as it went along. In war movies the main character always called his girlfriend so I called Debbie in Cincinnati.

I'd met Debbie while I was stationed in Rhode Island for storekeeper school several months earlier. We had only exchanged a few letters since then, but Debbie was the closest thing to a girlfriend I had. I'd dreamed once that I'd asked Debbie to write me while I was in Vietnam. In the dream she hemmed and hawed until her cheery, laughing face turned pale and amorphous and I felt desperately alone.

The phone booth was hot, so I kept the door open. That meant there was no light, and I dropped my change all over the steel floor. When I finally got through to her, I told Debbie about the dream. She promised that she would write. I blubbered something into the receiver and ended the conversation crying.

When I returned to the table, Stew was slumped forward, his left forearm in a puddle of beer and wet napkins. The Gerk was just staring into the distance saying, "A northern dictionary, Jesus Christ, a northern dictionary."

At the end of the night we all just stared at the table, our bellies bloated and our minds dulled. We shared a cab ride back to the base and I passed out on my bed.

The next day we assembled on the grinder, a cement yard across the road from our barracks. We loaded our backpacks and sea bags into trucks. Slowly we boarded buses parked nearby. Men with families lingered saying whatever men going to war say to their loved ones. When everyone was aboard we left for the airport.

As we pulled away, a young, blond woman and her little daughter waved good-bye to someone in the bus. She wore a tight-fitting yellow blouse, white shorts, and sunglasses. Her body was a rich golden tan. The little girl was also tan with blond hair and looked to be about three years old. Just before the bus turned the corner near the chow hall, the young woman turned away, picked up her daughter and began to cry. I didn't feel anything. I couldn't.

I never imagined going to Vietnam could be like this, a Sunday drive along the beach. We drove behind a family in a shiny red Mustang convertible, their seats filled with towels and bottles of suntan lotion, everyone wearing sunglasses and bathing suits, just enjoying the day, only dimly aware of the olive drab bus full of young men approaching from behind them.

I wondered about what kind of a farewell this was for men about to give their lives for their country? Where were the bands, the patriotic speeches and our grateful countrymen reaching out to touch us? Suddenly I wanted someone in a car to pull alongside and ask us where we were going.

"Vietnam," I'd answer loudly, and their expression would change to amazement and then gratitude.

"Give 'em hell and come home safe," they would reply. "I'll be praying for you."

A sign on a restaurant read, "Y'all come in."

"I'm sorry, I can't," I wanted to say. "I don't have time. You see, I'm going to Vietnam and I can't be late."

A half-hour later we pulled off the coastal highway and drove to a small, deserted, civilian airport.

A giant steel replica of our mascot the Seabee, a bumblebee with a wrench, shovel, and hammer in each of its three right hands and a machine gun in its left hands, was perched on a stand in front of the modest two-story terminal building. The mascot was stenciled on our uniforms and sometimes I felt like I was walking around with Mickey Mouse on my pocket. I couldn't relate to it. I was a writer, not a soldier-mechanic, and I didn't know how to use a machine gun any more than I knew how to run a backhoe.

We pulled onto a field near the terminal building and waited for the plane. The heat and cigarette fumes in the bus became unbearable and, one by one, we went out to stretch.

Some of the wives had followed the bus in their cars and now the men were saying a second good-bye.

Lieutenant Kettles, the Officer-in-Charge, stood near the bus with his hands on his hips and glared through his gold rimmed sunglasses

"God dammit," he muttered, shaking his head and drawing his lips tight in disapproval. "They were supposed to say good-bye back at the base. God dammit, I told my wife to stay there. Why couldn't they?"

Nobody tried to stop them.

Finally the big silver Air Force C-141 lumbered in lazily from the north, banked widely and then started a slow descent. The plane seemed to hang in the air for a long time before it screeched down on the runway and taxied to a halt in front of us looking like a huge, tired bird, its long wings drooping halfway to the ground.

After the forward hatch whined open, the flight crew emerged wearing tight fitting fatigues with hooks and zippers.

The twin cargo bay doors in back of the plane opened and the crew began loading pallets of rifle boxes and field packs with a forklift.

The airfield was getting hot and I looked forward to being on board the plane and out of the sun. Finally everything was loaded and we began boarding. After I pulled myself up a short ladder, a burst of hot air from inside the plane rushed into my lungs. I shivered. This is insane, I thought. I'm gonna be roasted before I get to 'Nam.

I made my way through the fuselage and down two steps to the main cabin. The only two windows were on either side of the plane in the rear near the cargo, a neatly arranged pile of boxes on metal pallets covered with a yellow, webbed net. The net was fastened to rings on the pallet with large metal clips. Wires and metal tubes ran overhead, and black rubber bags containing emergency oxygen masks hung like sleeping bats from the fuselage next to each man.

There were six seats in each row, all facing the rear with a narrow aisle down the middle. I tried to ignore the suffocating heat as I climbed into a seat near the wall and fastened my seat belt. After the rest of the cargo was loaded, the massive double doors in the tail whined shut. I was soaked with sweat and felt like I was in a tomb. Finally the air vents near my feet began pouring cool, fresh air over my body. My ears popped as the cabin pressurized and the four jet engines began to scream. I took a deep breath and relaxed for the first time in days. The part of me that had left returned and I felt whole again.

Suddenly Gulfport didn't seem to exist anymore. I was being reincarnated as an egg in the belly of a great metal bird — my previous life was irrelevant. My identity would be determined by the challenges ahead. I felt the vibration of the engines against the back of my legs and a force tugging me forward as we raced down the runway.

The massive jet engines roared out a final good-bye as we jerked skyward. We climbed swiftly and leveled off at 30,000 feet. Eight hours later we landed in Anchorage, Alaska to refuel, then flew another eight hours to Okinawa.

A gentle wafting breeze of cool air from the vents near my seat put me to sleep as we finished the last leg of our journey to Vietnam, rendering me totally unprepared for what was to come.

17
DA NANG, VIETNAM
May 1967

FIVE HOURS OUT of Okinawa we began our descent into a jungle country with a tranquil-looking shoreline, turquoise lagoons and lush tropical foliage. We came in low over a broad bay and then banked steeply toward an area of olive drab buildings and silver quonset huts. My ears popped as the cabin depressurized and the plane began its final approach to the runway.

After we landed we taxied to the terminal and stopped. The cargo doors opened and a blast of hot, moist air and a blinding tropical light hit me in the face. The heat was worse than Gulfport.

The first person that I noticed after I got off the plane was a tall, lean, sun-blackened man with a droopy brown mustache, a faded cap and aviator sunglasses. He stood in the back of a long, open cargo truck. The stock of a double-barreled shotgun rested on his knee, as he waited for the pallets to be unloaded. Naked from the waist up, he had two bandoleers of shotgun shells crisscrossed over his chest and looked like a Mexican bandit.

I stared up at him and said, "You from Fifty-Eight?"

"Yep," he said, barely turning his head. "Welcome to Vietnam."

"Thanks," I said wiping the sweat from my face.

A forklift rolled across the tarmac and deposited a yellow webbed pallet of sea bags onto the bed of the deuce-and-a-half (2½ ton truck).

"Hop in the front seat and I'll give you a ride to the base," he said.

I climbed up into the passenger seat, shivered from the heat then burned my elbow on the metal door.

"Ouch," I said and pulled my arm back in.

The bandit climbed in, started the engine and put out his hand.

"Howdy, I'm Tex."

"I'm Richard," I said shaking his hand.

"You wouldn't happen to be a storekeeper, would you?"

"I sure am. What are you," I asked, thinking that maybe he was a Marine.

"I'm a storekeeper, too."

"So what's with the shotgun and ammo?" I asked. "You think we're gonna get attacked on the way to the base?"

"You never know," said Tex. "The fuckin' gooks could hit us anytime." I didn't know what to think. Maybe he was just trying to scare me — the green replacement just off the plane.

We drove out the main gate of the airfield and onto a newly paved asphalt road heading for Camp Haskins South, where Mobile Construction Battalion 58 was eagerly awaiting our arrival. Before getting off the plane, I had pictured our base as cantonments of huts hacked out of the jungle and surrounded by barbed wire and guard towers. I wasn't prepared for the immensity of the American military presence. We drove by miles of bases, warehouses, hangers, airfields, and fuel tanks. There were acres of lumberyards and ammo dumps. Interspersed between the bases were clusters of tin-roofed Vietnamese huts almost hidden behind broad-leafed palm trees.

We rounded a bend in the road and saw a military truck parked in front of a Vietnamese house on our right. A dozen young men dressed in tee-shirts, shorts and sneakers sat in the back. They looked like college kids on a beach outing. Tex slowed the truck and pointed.

"Skivey house."

"What's a skivey house?"

Tex smiled. "That's a place where GI's get boom-boom."

Just then a young man ran out of the house and everyone started cheering. He jumped into the truck and they were off.

When we left Gulfport on a Sunday we flew against the clock, so it was still Sunday when we landed. Troops were relaxing on their half-day off. Beach Boys music blared from Sony tape decks, "She'll have fun, fun, fun 'til her Daddy takes her T-bird away. . . ." Men stood around in faded uniform cut-offs and boots, holding cans of Budweiser, wearing floppy jungle hats, and waving as we passed. I began to relax. So this is what everyone had been afraid of. It seemed like Vietnam was going to be one giant beach party.

Suddenly, I felt we were going to win the war. We would pave the way for a prosperous Vietnam, build expensive hotels on this bay and provide jobs. We did it in Europe, in the South Pacific, in Korea, and we could do it in Vietnam. How could we lose? We had the organization and the manpower. We had millions of dollars in infrastructure. But most of all, we had the Beach Boys filling the air with American music and values.

When we got to the base everyone was glad to see us because that meant they were going home soon. After we were assigned huts and stowed our gear, we were treated to a steak dinner on the grill with lots of beer to wash it down. After a couple beers I began to feel faint. Maybe it was the heat. I eased up and started drinking Coke.

The next day I explored my new surroundings. The base had basketball courts, showers, ten-man huts, an outdoor movie theater, a PX and clubs overlooking a broad tropical beach. The library was an air-conditioned metal quonset hut. The Seabees also built a dispensary, a post office and a modern looking A-frame chapel. We had a souvenir shack and laundry on base run by a Vietnamese man and his three daughters.

During the day the temperature rose to 120 degrees, so we were advised to take salt tablets and drank enormous quantities of water to combat fluid loss. Rivulets of perspiration ran into my eyes and poured onto my sheets when I tried to rest on my cot during lunch hour. After a week in country my crotch got hit with jungle rot rash and I scratched until I bled. Then came the migraine headaches. How could I last another nine months? I started counting the days, but that only depressed me. There were too many of them.

Soon I learned to live a day at a time. My body acclimated itself to the weather. My jungle rot left when I stopped wearing underwear. I realized that it could have been a lot worse. I could have been a grunt in the field wading through putrid swamps or trying not to step on the enemy's hidden feces coated bamboo spikes.

The actual fighting seemed far away. Armored personnel carriers traveled the main roads going to and from the field, and helicopter gun ships cruised low along the beach. I could see aircraft carriers on the horizon and occasionally, destroyers bombarded the valley on the other side of the mountains west of our base. Sometimes after work we'd sit on the beach sipping beer as Navy jets made bombing runs on enemy positions in the distant hills. They dove in from the clouds like hawks, then pulled up and released their napalm canisters, arcing them toward the target. As the canisters exploded, we'd see a puff of black smoke and then wait for the low rumble.

Occasionally the mortar alert siren went off at night. We jumped into the mortar pits next to our huts, but never got hit. Other bases miles away got hit, but never ours while I was there.

I worked in the air-conditioned Material Liaison Office (MLO) trying to keep an accurate inventory of the supply yard. Invariably lumber and sheet metal were stolen or traded to Marine or Army units in the field. Many of these units had very little supply support from their regiments, so I didn't mind a few trades. I just wrote them off as "Loss by Inventory." However, this created a problem prior to our annual supply inspection. Mr. Baker was the MLO officer, a handsome young ensign from Texas with dark hair and a ruddy complexion. We worked in the same office and had a friendly, yet formal relationship. One day Baker asked me to inventory a bin of circuit breakers. I couldn't find them. When I told Baker, he asked everyone to leave the office. I knew I was in trouble.

Baker leaned back in his chair and looked wistfully out the Plexiglas window into the warehouse where wooden shipping crates were stacked.

He looked back at me and said, "Chamberlin, you aren't really a storekeeper, are you?"

"No, I'm not," I said. "I wanted to be a journalist, but they made me a storekeeper instead. I didn't want to crawl through slime and get my ass shot off. If I went to Vietnam, I wanted to work in an air-conditioned office and sip beer and watch jets drop napalm on the Viet Cong. I'm sorry about the inventory."

Here it comes, I thought.

Baker's lips turned up on one side as if he was about to smile but couldn't quite pull it off. He let out a sigh, stared at his desk for a moment then rolled his eyes upward. He smiled broadly and began to laugh.

"You know, Chamberlin, I had this bird dog back home . . . used to take him hunting for quail . . . spent a lot of time teaching him to bring back the bird once I shot it. One day we were out in a swamp and I had just shot a quail. Old Blue, that was the dog's name, went into the swamp and didn't come out."

I was glad he wasn't chewing me out, but wondered where he was going with this.

"I looked around for him and called his name, but he didn't come. It was gettin' dark so I walked back to the house and there he was, chewin' on the head of this bird. I goddamn near split a gut over that one. I guess he just figured he'd get one for himself."

We both laughed. "Well, just do your job the best you can," he said, grabbing his hat from a hook on the wall. He walked out the door shaking his head and smiling. I figured he wasn't really a supply officer and I wasn't really a storekeeper. Existentially I was a writer and he was a quail hunter. We were both just trapped in someone else's version of reality.

☯

Sunday afternoons after paydays I'd occasionally catch a ride to the main PX, about three miles away on the main coastal highway. Americans built the road to facilitate troop movement, but everyone used it. I got a ride with some Seabees who were going to the main PX to buy Japanese camera equipment for half the normal price.

We left after lunch and drove south along the newly paved asphalt road. The road smelled like hot tar and heat mirages rose from the surface. An old *mamasan* carried massive bundles of firewood to the market. The bundles were suspended from a yoke resting on her shoulders. Half running, as if she were about to trip, but never tripping, she rhythmically bounced the load along. She wore loose fitting black pants and was barefoot, her flat leathery feet kicking up dust from the red clay along the shoulder of the road. A man who was urinating in his garden glanced up casually as the old woman passed.

As we got closer to the center of town two young women in white silk blouses walked along holding hands. Across the road a heavily made-up prostitute beckoned to me.

"Hey, GI, me boom-boom you! Only five dollars MPC. We have good time." MPC's were Military Pay Certificates. We weren't supposed to use them off base, but Vietnamese merchants accepted them anyway. Every so often the color of the currency was changed making the old ones worthless to civilians. The Vietnamese would panic and crowd around the main gate, trying to sell them back to us for pennies on the dollar.

The prostitute leaned against the opening to her shanty, its roof tiled with flattened beer cans. In the shade of the house next door an old man wearing only shorts squatted as he hammered on a foot-long copper shell casing, skillfully shaping it into a vase.

At times it seemed like the entire population was living off our garbage. Groups of children scurried around like tiny insects and we veered to avoid running them over. The warm, thick odor of burning sandalwood filled the air. A dump truck tipped its load of scrap lumber as people swarmed forward to grab the precious refuse.

The road narrowed as we got closer to downtown Da Nang. People wearing broad, cone-shaped bamboo hats were everywhere, making the crowded street resemble a place of spinning tops. Bikes and scooters weaved dangerously close to yellow and red busses.

On the other side of town we reached our destination, a series of married Butler Buildings (metal barns built together in a row). We parked the jeep and went inside where there was a long cement floor with rows of military supplies stacked on wooden pallets. There were also commercial products like soap, magazines, snack foods, blue jeans, underwear and picnic supplies. The building contained a beachhead of American culture in a land being transformed by the desire for modern material goods. Although it was just a military PX, to the Vietnamese it was like Saks Fifth Avenue.

18
SINGAPORE FLING
October 1967

ABOUT HALF WAY THROUGH our deployment, Uncle Sam offered us a free vacation to one of several Asian cities. Officially it was called R&R (Rest and Recreation). Unofficially it was I&I (Intercourse and Intoxication). I looked forward to leaving Vietnam for a few days but was apprehensive about the intercourse part because I was still a virgin.

I had tried to get laid several times but without much luck. I almost had sex with a girl in my senior year of high school, but her fiancée hit town early, found out about us and gave her a black eye. Another time a pimp in the Cuban section of downtown Miami tried to interest me in a prostitute who reminded me of a heavily made up orangutan. I wasn't buying.

I chose Singapore for R&R because the name sounded exciting, as in *The Road to Singapore* or a Singapore Sling. Singapore conjured up images of swashbucklers and sailing ships, Errol Flynn and sultry tropical nights.

Before we left for R&R we had a lecture on the perils of unprotected sexual intercourse. The talk was held in the chapel and the podium was a small raised platform with a large crucifix behind it. The job of helping us keep our sexual organs clean fell to the corpsmen, or penis machinists as they were sometimes called.

Rather than needlessly confuse Seabees with arcane medical terminology, the lecture was delivered in the vernacular.

"Now I know that some of you men have already been on R&R," the corpsman began. He was a lifer first-class petty officer with a sneer and a droopy mustache. He talked in an accusatory voice, as if everyone in the room had already contracted every venereal disease from Hamburg to Hong Kong.

"And if you're like most of the assholes out there you probably don't use any rubbers, so God help you when you get back home." He paused, waiting for the effect to sink in. There were a few nervous chuckles. Some men lit cigarettes.

"Has anyone out there ever heard of the bull-headed clap?" he asked. No one raised their hand.

"Well, I'll tell ya what it is. When ya get normal clap your dick hurts and you piss out a lot of pus. We can give you a shot in the ass and that'll take care of it." He put his hand on his hips and paced back and forth with his head down.

He looked up at the audience and in a lowered voice said, "But there's a new strain of clap out there. There's no cure for it. We've tried all kinds of antibiotics, but it's immune to them all. When I was with the fleet in Yokohama we had this sailor who had the bull-headed clap. You know why they call it the bull-headed clap?" He looked around. "We call it the bull-headed clap because your dick swells up like a big black bullfrog."

There was more nervous laughter. I imagined a sailor lying in bed with this huge black, festering growth where his penis had been.

"So you assholes think it's funny? Well, I hope to God that you never get it because if you do, you can kiss the United States good-bye. The Navy can't ship you home. You're a health menace, so all's you do is float around the ocean with a big, black, swollen dick until you die." The lecture was over.

From the back of the quonset hut, the furious voice of Master Chief Petty Officer Simon Peter Gray bellowed. "I want you men to fall in outside, in two ranks, immediately."

I wondered what we did to offend the elder master chief. His face was red and he was furious.

"I have never in my life seen such an utter disregard for the sanctity of a sacred spot," he shouted. Even though I wasn't religious I had to agree that the language the corpsman used was inappropriate in a church.

"I don't know where you men were brought up, but smoking in the Lord's House is blasphemy." With the word blasphemy, he walked down the ranks staring each sinner in the eye. When he reached the end of the line, he turned in disgust and shouted, "Dismissed."

I wondered why the Senior Chief regarded smoking in church as more sacrilegious than using foul language and disgusting images.

The day we left for Singapore, I donned my white sailor uniform for the first time in months. I tied my black scarf several times before I got the two tips to hang down evenly. For the final touch, I ran my thumbs along the upper rim of my white sailor hat until the edges curved slightly outward. When I finished, I looked in the mirror. With my tropical tan and newly sprouted mustache I looked positively stunning.

We flew out of Da Nang on a commercial airliner, a full complement of hell-raising, sex-hungry young soldiers and sailors.

It was a short trip to Singapore compared with our flight from the States. When we landed we were briefed on local customs and the rules of conduct governing American servicemen. After that, I took a cab to my hotel.

Singapore was as hot as Vietnam, so I spent most of the day inside or lounging around the swimming pool with the other servicemen.

That night I went to the hotel lounge. All the GI's were in civvies, and if not for the Asian bar girls in sexy, satin dresses, the scene could have been mistaken for a fraternity party. I had a couple Singapore Slings to loosen up and then started fast dancing with one of the girls. She had dark skin and huge, brown eyes lined heavily with mascara. Her long, straight, black hair hung down to the top of her well-rounded butt. I found her very attractive and decided to proposition her, but wasn't sure how to do it.

When the music was over, the band switched to a slow song. We danced again, gently swaying to the music. What to do now? I didn't want to seem overly aggressive. Slowly I let my hand drift downward and cupped it over her fanny. She didn't respond. I held her closer and her breasts pressed against my chest. After the music stopped I noticed a heavy-set, older woman with an embroidered pink muu-muu and hair drawn back in a bun. Girls at the other end of the bar surrounded her. I decided she must be the *mamasan*, the person I had to make a deal with to get a girl.

I walked around the bar and stood next to her. She looked up.

"Ah, I'd like to, ah, take one of your girls to my room," I said.

"You want girl? Which girl?"

I pointed to the girl I had been dancing with.

"You give me one hundred dollars and you take girl upstairs."

One hundred dollars seemed like an awful lot of money to me. I hesitated.

"One hundred dollars Singapore money same-same thirty US," she said, anticipating my objection.

It still seemed like a lot of money. I began to bargain.

"I'll give you fifty," I said.

The girls around her giggled, "You go to another bar. Maybe you find girl for fifty dollars." There were more giggles. "Here you pay one hundred dollars Singapore."

What the hell, I thought. What was I doing, saving for my retirement? I reached inside my wallet and gave her a hundred dollars Singapore.

The next dance was different. The girl kissed my lips passionately and fondled my crotch. I wasn't prepared for this abrupt change. It seemed so artificial.

I gently pushed her away and looked into her eyes.

"So what's your name?" I asked.

"Jeannie. What's yours?"

"Richard," I answered. "Where are you from?"

"My father was Portuguese. My mother from India. I now from Singapore. Where you from, Richard?"

"I'm from Miami," I said, then added, "Have you ever heard of it?"

"Sure have," she said enthusiastically. "Miami very romantic."

I held her closer and started to relax.

"Yeah, I grew up in Miami. I've got two sisters. They're still in high school," I said. I didn't know why I was telling her this. Why would she care? I felt stupid.

We made some more small talk and then she introduced me to her girlfriend who was with Guns Duluth, a tall, lanky, Huey helicopter gunner from the Mekong Delta.

The two girls decided they wanted to see a movie. I went along with the idea even though I was tired. The movie was the James Bond flick, *Doctor No,* with Chinese subtitles. I dozed off in the theater.

After the movie we went back to the hotel.

As we walked through the lobby, the young clerk called us over. He had to check Jeannie's health card.

The clerk gave it a quick look, handed it back, and said. "Card okay. You have good time."

"I hate that," said Jeannie. "They always hassle us."

We got into the elevator. I was very, very tired. My body felt heavy and all I wanted to do was sleep.

We walked into my room and I locked the door. I grabbed Jeannie and gave her a long hard kiss, trying to feign passion. She pulled away.

"Your mustache," she said. "It tickles."

I ran my fingers over the two-month old growth above my upper lip. "Whadaya mean it tickles?" I said. "It didn't bother you at the bar."

"Why don't you shave it off?" she suggested.

Shave it off, I thought? I'd grown it to look sexy, but if the woman I was about to have sex with didn't want me to have one, I could shave it. I grabbed my shaving kit, walked over to the sink, lathered up and shaved it off. After I patted my face dry with a towel, she gave me a quick kiss.

"Now you look more sexy," she said, smiling.

"Let's take a shower," I suggested. I needed more stimulation to get in the mood.

"I don't want to take a shower," she said. "I don't have my hair drier with me." She took off her dress, then her red slip, and put it over the lamp next to the bed. "This will make it more romantic," she said as she crawled into bed and took off her panties and bra. I had a condom in my drawer and wondered if it was time to put it on, but since I had never used one I felt awkward. I hoped she'd been tested for bull-headed clap.

This wasn't working out like I wanted it to. I hadn't even seen her naked and now I'm supposed to have sex with her? But it seemed there was nothing left to do but go along with her. I peeled off my pants and underwear and crawled on top of her. She spread her legs. I waited for nature to jump-start me. Nothing happened.

"I'm sorry, I guess I'm just tired," I muttered.

I was cool on the outside, but inside my ego was imploding. What was wrong with me? I fondled her breasts and kissed her lips, but nothing worked. Jeannie turned over and went to sleep. I stayed awake, pulled the sheets up and peeked at her body from time to time. All I could see was her back, the curve of her dark buttocks and her legs drawn up against her chest.

I felt like a failure. In the morning she left and I spent the next few days getting drunk. When I got back to Vietnam, my failure was still eating away at me. I just had to share it with someone. I was at the enlisted men's club one night having a beer with a guy named Buzzy who was a truck driver from Alpha Company. Buzzy was a short guy with a self deprecating sense of humor who liked to talk about coon hunting on his parents' farm in Tennessee.

"So how'd you like Singapore?" he asked me.

"Sure was hot," I said. "And the girls were expensive, being a port city and all that."

"Yeah, not like here," he said.

I waited a minute and thought what the hell. "I got something to tell ya Buzzy," I said. "I don't want this to get around, okay?"

"Don't worry. What's on your mind?"

"Well, the first night I got to Singapore I paid about thirty bucks for this girl at a bar and . . . we went up to my room and . . . well . . . I was really tired from the trip and everything, and I . . . I . . . just couldn't do it. I don't know what happened. I just couldn't do it." I stared out at the lights of a carrier stationed off the coast. It seemed desolate and very far away.

"Shit man, don't worry," he said. He drained his beer can, crushed it on the table and threw it on the beach. "It happens to everyone once in a while." He got up, gave me a slap on the back.

"Don't worry. It'll be okay," he said again before he turned to go back to his hootch.

I wanted to embrace him. I was back in the community of men.

On January 30, 1968, shortly before we came home, the Tet Offensive began. The North Vietnamese and the Viet Cong, who were supposed to have been weakened by our intensive bombing, launched massive attacks on several key cities. Fighting was especially intense in Saigon to the south of us and in Hue to the north. Luckily our base was untouched. The offensive was quickly beaten back and the enemy suffered enormous casualties. Yet, the fact that the North was able to launch such a large offensive was a turning point.

Americans began to wonder whether the tremendous expense of the war was worth it. Battered by anti-war protests,

President Johnson, on March 31, addressed the nation and announced that he would not run again for the Presidency. He began to seek a negotiated peace, cut back the bombing of North Vietnam, and rejected requests from his generals for more troops.

As the time neared to deploy back to the states, short-timer calendars appeared on the walls in the huts and offices. Often the calendars depicted nude women, their bodies sectioned off like cuts of meat, and numbered in descending order of days remaining with the number "1" most frequently occupying a region of male fascination.

When the advanced party from the relieving battalion arrived, we had only thirty days left. Our military bearing and dress deteriorated. We stopped wearing uniforms. The practice was so rampant that the officers just ignored it.

The day we left, we loaded our gear into trucks and headed for the air base. When the big, silver, C-141 landed on the runway, it was one of the happiest days of my life. In the back of my mind I knew I'd have to make one more deployment to Vietnam, but for now, as I walked toward the plane, I was going home at last and it seemed like my feet no longer touched the ground.

19
BACK TO THE WORLD
Gulfport – January 1968

TWENTY-FOUR HOURS and two refueling stops later, we touched down in Biloxi. As we got off the plane a Navy band played *The Stars and Stripes Forever*. Families waved small American flags and kissed their men. I felt awkward because I didn't deserve the adulation. I had kept records of supplies that were lost or stolen, watched as jets bombed distant hills, flown to Singapore and gotten drunk. I didn't deserve the band. I was just glad to be back.

The next day I went into town and, while waiting for a bus, entertained myself by staring at cars driving along the coastal highway. The road was a kaleidoscope of color. There were pink El Dorado Cadillacs and white Lincoln Continentals. There were fire engine red MG's and aquamarine Pontiac Catalinas with gleaming chrome bumpers and hubcaps.

Such affluence! What made it more amazing was that mechanics and waitresses and salesmen and housewives drove most of these cars. The drivers were teenagers who worked at fast food shops and motel clerks and bus drivers and bartenders. Americans have so much and they don't even realize it, I thought. My eyes settled on a girl in a miniskirt climbing off the bus as I got on. My sex drive came back in a flash.

Grocery stores sold several brands of the same thing. At the PX in 'Nam, one brand of toothpaste seemed all right. I put it on my toothbrush, stuck it inside my mouth, it tasted like mint and that was okay. I never thought I was deprived. This world of affluence was not my world anymore. This disconnect with my culture would grow and fester as time went on causing me to resent the great emphasis Americans put on material wealth. The waste of energy involved in the competition between manufacturers of the same product seemed obscene.

When it was time to go on leave, I decided it would be nice to see Debbie Kingston in Cincinnati and then swing over to Jeffersonville, Indiana to visit my family. Debbie was the woman I had called from Mary's bar the night before I left for Vietnam. We had dated while I was in storekeeper school in Newport, Rhode Island and we exchanged a few letters while I was in Vietnam. I called her and she invited me up for a visit.

I took a bus to Cincinnati and checked into a hotel. She picked me up in her father's Cadillac greeting me with a warm hug. She looked very preppie wearing a Navy blue blazer and plaid culottes with matching knee socks.

"Nice to see you again," she said.

"Same here."

"How long will you be in town?"

"I'm not sure," I said. "I'm going to visit my family in Indiana at some point."

"Good," she said. "Is there something you want to do?"

"I'd like to see Mount Adams. I heard that's a cool place to visit."

She wrinkled up her nose. "It's not really the kind of place I want to go."

"What's wrong with it?"

"There's a lot of hippies and pot there. It's not a proper place for ladies."

I remembered she was very much the lady and that's what attracted me to her, but now she seemed a bit snobbish.

"I just wanted to see how the country has changed since I've been gone." I said. "I read about hippies and anti-war demonstrations and thought it would be interesting to check out the scene."

"There's a lot better places to go than Mount Adams," she said.

We drove out to the country where her family lived in a restored mansion, just across the Ohio River near Covington, Kentucky. The house was lavishly furnished with oriental rugs, oak furniture and crystal chandeliers. Golden framed paintings of her ancestors decorated the wall.

Debbie introduced me to her father who was a doctor; a big, heavy set, balding man with gray hair. Just then the phone rang and Debbie excused herself to take the call.

Dr. Kingston invited me into his den where he had a roaring blaze going in the fireplace. He sat down in a large padded chair and lit up a cigar.

"Cigar?" he said, offering me one.

"No thanks."

I sat opposite him on a red, velvet couch.

"Well here, let me pour you a martini," he said getting up and going to the bar.

"That's okay, really," I said.

"Nonsense," He said. "We've got to celebrate your visit." He mixed up the drinks, brought me a glass, then sat back down.

"Debbie tells me you were in the Army."

"Actually it was the Navy."

"Good for you. My father was an admiral in the Navy. That's his picture behind you."

I turned around and saw a dark painting of a scowling naval officer with an ornamental sword at his side.

"After he retired we bought this land," he said. "This used to be tobacco plantation. We've got forty acres and some stables. I used to raise race horses as a hobby, but it just got to be too much. The kids weren't interested so after the last one went to pasture I didn't buy any more. We decided to put money into fixing up the house. I installed a swimming pool in the back and my wife started a greenhouse. She raises roses. Do you like flowers?"

"Yeah. Flowers are great."

"Every year she enters them in a contest we have at the country club. Last year she got runner-up. I think we've got to start them earlier this year; they're so temperamental," he went on, then paused to drain his glass.

I was wearing a tweed sport coat and a black, wool Navy watch sweater. The room was heating up and I began sweating heavily.

"Another drink?" he asked.

"Sure," I said, hoping another drink would help me cool off.

"So what do you do in the Army?" he asked, handing me another glass.

"I'm in the Navy and I just got back from Vietnam," I said. He was beginning to annoy me.

"Oh yes, sorry. Well, it must be good to be home. What are your plans now? Are you going to college?"

I was hungry now. Why didn't their maid offer me some hors d'oeuvres?

"I've got another deployment to make," I said. "Then I'll probably be transferred to another duty station because I still have two-and-a-half years left in my enlistment."

He lit up another cigar. I found it hard to breathe. I wondered if he was testing me. He wanted to determine whether or not I'd fit into the family. If I married his daughter I'd have to spend every Sunday evening talking about racehorses and roses with him and choking on cigar smoke. Eventually I'd be expected to start toking up on a stogie myself. Maybe he just wanted to drive me away from his daughter. I started getting a migraine headache. He rambled on about the stables and the swimming pool and the veranda and the rose gardens.

Finally Debbie came in and suggested we go to the grocery store and pick up some things for dinner. I excused myself.

When Debbie insisted that I drive the Cadillac, I felt embarrassed, like a complete impostor. After dinner we walked around her father's private hunting grounds and she showed me foundations of the old slave quarters. That evening she drove me back to my hotel.

"Do you want to come in for a while?" I asked. "I've got some pictures from Vietnam I can show you." The pictures were an excuse. What I really wanted was to be alone with her for a while. I wanted a woman in my arms.

"Well, I really should be going," she said. "We can do something tomorrow."

"Oh, come on. Just for a little while."

She parked the car and we went inside.

I got the pictures out and we sat on my bed looking at them.

"What's this?" she asked pointing to a bunker.

"That's an old cement bunker left over from the Fifties when Ho Chi Minh fought against the French," I said, scooting next to her. "When the Americans came, we built a sandbag bunker right on top of it, for better visibility I suppose." I gave her a little hug.

We looked at a few more pictures. "How long were you there again?" asked Debby.

"Nine months."

"That's a long time."

"It sure is. I missed you," I lied, and kissed her on the cheek.

She turned toward me and I kissed her on the lips. I put my arms around her and we held each other for a moment, then I stretched out on the bed and she lay down next to me.

"I can't stay long," she said.

I kissed her a couple more times. Something wasn't right. I felt uncomfortable and sat up.

"Yeah, I guess you better go," I said. "I'm pretty tired after the bus trip and everything."

She got her purse and I walked her out to the Cadillac.

"It was nice seeing you, Richard. Would you like to go shopping with me tomorrow and look at some Persian rugs?"

"Yeah. Persian rugs, great."

The next morning I left her a note with the desk clerk and took a cab to the bus station. I caught a Greyhound to Jeffersonville, Indiana where my family had moved after renting out our house in Miami. My father had a temporary job selling hearing aids and my mother was teaching piano to poor, black kids in the nearby Louisville, Kentucky public schools. My oldest sister, Bette, was just finishing up high school and my younger sister, Sandra, was still a freshman.

My maternal grandmother had recently passed away, and my parents used my mother's share of the inheritance to buy eighty acres of undeveloped land near Columbia, South Carolina.

It was a dream come true for them. My dad had learned how to sell land working for other people, but by now they had their own business. They called it Forest Manor and planned on subdividing it into half-acre parcels for mobile homes.

My father, Harlow, was born into a Methodist household in 1906 in the small former logging town of Loyal, Wisconsin. His parents weren't particularly religious and he began to question church dogma at an early age. By the time he was twenty, he'd become an atheist.

In 1959 my father did something that changed our lives forever. He sued the public schools for bible reading. The impetus for the suit began when my sister Sandra came home from North Miami Elementary school in tears. Her first grade teacher had told her people who didn't believe in God were going to hell. Since we were atheists, she took that very personally. When my mother complained to the principal, he suggested she send her daughter to a private school. My parents asked the American Civil Liberties Union for advice. What began as an inappropriate comment by a principal ended up in a precedent-setting lawsuit against the Dade County Public School system for violation of the constitutional separation between church and state.

As a result of the publicity surrounding the case, my dad lost his job as a salesman for a major radio station. After the Florida State Supreme Court upheld the law, the case was appealed to the United States Supreme Court. But before it got there, the justices ruled against school prayer in a similar case. In 1964 the case was referred back to Florida where the state court justices were obligated to rule in our favor. There was no monetary gain — only a cease and desist order to the Florida Public Schools.

Four years later my dad was still paying the price for standing up for his beliefs. He hustled up sales jobs and the family got by.

The first night after I arrived in Jeffersonville my dad and I were up late talking after my mother and sisters had gone to bed. The house was dark and the only light came from a low-hanging lamp over his head. I sat on a couch on the other side of the room.

"Well, how's the hearing aid job going?" I asked.

"Aw, hells bells," he said, swatting the air with the back of his hand. "I've made a few sales, but not really enough. They gave me Northern Kentucky."

He took a drag on his Viceroy, which was advertised as the thinking man's cigarette. As he exhaled, I watched the smoke curl up toward the light.

"Those goddamn hillbillies," he said. "I was back in . . . hell, somewhere in the sticks. I got this ignorant old man to try on a hearing aid. When I turned it up for him, his eyes bugged out like a frog, he jumped up pointing his finger at me and yelled, 'devil'."

My dad rose from his chair and pointed his finger, acting out the scene.

"I tried to explain that it was like a radio that amplified sound, but he just came at me yelling that it was the machinations of Satan. I got the hell out of there in a hurry," he laughed and sat down.

I laughed with him. There was a moment of quiet. He seemed small and vulnerable, trying to laugh away his troubles. I felt like giving him a hug, but I remained seated. The only physical contact we ever had was a handshake.

"Yeah," I said. "There's a lot of ignorance in them thar hills."

"It's that goddamn religion," he said. He took another drag on his cigarette and began quoting an unnamed author. "Man, by his godlike nature, is the only creature who sees things not as they are, but as he would like them to be." He paused and then went on, sounding like a college professor.

"Language has given man a tool for astounding accomplishments, but he has also been victimized by the same tool. Man and man alone can create concepts that don't exist. Does anybody today believe the world is flat, or of the mythical centaur or of mermaids?"

"Well, I guess you could prove that those things really don't exist," I said. "I mean, no one has ever pulled a mermaid out of the water and put her on the six-o-clock news." I reconsidered my statement. "But just because you don't see a mermaid, doesn't necessarily mean that she doesn't exist. Maybe just nobody has seen one."

"Well, if you can't sense something, how do you know it exists?" he responded. "A religionist is like a man who goes into a pitch dark room and says he can see a black cat."

"But, what if you can feel the black cat?" I said. "What if you just have an intuition there is a cat there?"

"Intuition isn't proof," he countered. "It's just a guess. If you turned on the lights, maybe a cat would be there and maybe it wouldn't. The great theological thinkers have duped the ignorant masses into thinking that the cat is there."

I hated it when he referred to the ignorant masses, like our family was somehow superior to everyone else. That attitude had set us apart from society while I was a teenager trying to fit in.

"Well, I don't know," I said, trying to pierce his armor of absolute reality. "A lot of people take comfort in religion. It gives them meaning in life. It provides a community, a place where they can be with their friends, you know, they donate stuff to charity and. . . ." My voice trailed off.

"That's fine, but it doesn't stop there. Next thing you know they want everyone to believe in an anthropomorphic god just like they do. And if you don't . . . well . . ." he paused, "you're somehow evil or lost or you need to be persuaded. There have been more people killed in the name of religion than all the wars in history. It's a vicious, never ending cycle."

He wasn't about to give an inch, so I let the issue drop. Since my father spent a lot of time reading books about Einstein's theory of relativity he changed the subject and we began talking about traveling faster than the speed of light, time running backwards, and the atomic bomb. I never understood the mathematics of relativity, but I admired his intelligence. At times he would pause and slowly blow smoke rings into the air. I watched them slowly expand and then dissipate like dying supernovas. I figured his contemplation of the universe was as close as he would ever get to a religious experience. And that was pretty good, since religions probably began when our ancestors gazed into the night sky, enthralled with the majesty of what they saw.

After about a week visiting the family in Indiana I headed back to Gulfport. As time passed I began to realize there was a lot I didn't understand about the war. I had assumed that with over 500,000 troops we would eventually wear down the enemy. Yet, the war dragged on and on. I began to understand why after I read two books about the conflict. One book was *The Bitter Heritage* by Arthur Schlesinger. Schlesinger recommended that the United States put the burden of fighting the war on the South Vietnamese Army. That argument made sense to me because the more we did for them, the less they had to do for themselves. I also read Barbara Ward's *Rich Nations and Poor Nations* in which she argued that Vietnam was a nation emerging from its feudal age. The allegiance of the people was not to the central government, but to the village and the hamlet. The political consciousness necessary to present a unified front to the enemy was historically absent.

Eventually I began to believe we were going to lose the war even though America was the most powerful country in the world. How was it possible that we were actually going to be defeated by a peasant army from an undeveloped country? That idea was hard to accept, yet it seemed inevitable. What made it worse was that after spending billions of dollars on the war and suffering thousands of casualties, it appeared that the Johnson administration wasn't about to endure the embarrassment of an early withdrawal. We seemed destined to see the war through to the bloody end.

Even though I no longer believed in the war, after five months in Gulfport, I was heading back to 'Nam for the second time.

20
CHU LAI
June 1968

IN LATE SUMMER OF 1968 we redeployed to The Republic of Vietnam for eight more months. This time we were based in Chu Lai, about fifty miles south of Da Nang. We flew over in commercial airlines. When we arrived, cute stewardesses waved good-bye to us. As we walked down the ramp, one old Seabee veteran sighed and said, "What a way to go to war."

Although our arrival was different, everything else felt the same. Our camp was similar to the one in Da Nang. I knew I would have to relive all the long, hot, asshole months again. It was like we had never left, like we had arrived at the airport in Da Nang to go home and someone said, "Sorry, Chamberlin, you've gotta be here for another eight months!" There was the familiar acrid odor of burning excrement and kerosene as the latrines were cleaned out, the same energy-draining heat and humidity. There were the same wooden plank walkways over the sand between the huts, and the same sweet smell of hot tar as the roads approached their melting point beneath the tropical sun.

One thing that was new was our Chief Petty Officer in charge of the supply yard and warehouse. He was Master Chief

Pruitt, a slightly overweight man in his late fifties about to retire. He had good ol' boy-from-Tennessee charm, but it was only a ruse.

During our first week "in country," he gathered all the storekeepers together in his small, air-conditioned office. He stood behind a gray, bulky, government-issued desk and peered at us with hard, steady eyes.

"For the next eight months I'm going to be your father, your mother, your uncle, your boss and your god," he said. I was going to ask him if he wanted us to genuflect when we came into his office, but thought better of it.

"If you want anything," he went on, "come and see me. Everything is to be routed through me." I could see that this was going to be a long eight months.

I was in charge of the Shipping and Receiving Warehouse and the Pre-Positioned Camp Components (PPCC's). At the warehouse we received supplies and distributed them to the battalion. We also shipped out materials needed by other Seabee units in- country. The PPCC's were mostly rotting plywood crates containing everything a battalion would need to redeploy in an emergency. My job was to inventory the boxes, check their contents against a master list, and then have the material re-boxed or replaced.

I worked under a Second Class Storekeeper from Alabama named Mack. Mack kept a bottle of gin on the floor behind a high stack of boxes. He would start sneaking drinks in the morning and by noon he'd be passed out on the floor. At quitting time, I'd go behind the boxes and kick him in the boots to wake him up. He'd eat chow in the mess hall, go to the enlisted men's club and get drunk again. After the club closed, his drinking buddies would carry him back to the hut and throw him on his bed.

Mack preferred to use two mattresses — I'm not sure why, but it proved to be a disadvantage. Often during the night we'd hear a thud on the floor and someone would help Mack back to bed. After a few weeks we got tired of putting him back in bed and let him lie on the floor until morning.

One day he passed out at dinner and ended up in the dispensary where he went through the DT's for three days. He was sober for a while after he got back to the warehouse, but then resumed his drinking. In his absence, I became the de facto head of the Shipping and Receiving Department. I resented having to do Mack's job and one day took my frustrations out by spearing shipping crates with the forklift.

The tedium of the long days was occasionally broken by mortar alerts. When we first arrived in-country, we took the alerts seriously, jumping into the sandbagged mortar pit located just outside our huts and waiting for the all-clear siren. Like in Da Nang, we never got hit. Eventually we became cavalier about it, sitting around outside smoking and telling jokes until the alert was over.

The sirens went off one night shortly after the Shore Patrol deposited Mack on the floor beneath his bunk.

Oh shit! Not another alert, I thought. I got up and resigned myself to sitting in the mortar pit until the all-clear siren was sounded. Suddenly a Seabee from the security platoon burst in.

"Get your rifles and report to the gunner's mate hooch," he said. "This is not a drill."

What the hell? Why couldn't the sentries deal with this? I put on my steel helmet, grabbed my M-16 and unzipped its dust cover. We all ran to the hooch and were issued new, never-been-shot-at flack jackets and a couple of boxes of ammunition. I jammed eighteen of the sleek, precision-made, gold and silver rounds into each of my magazine clips, then put the clips into my pants pocket.

When I ran back to the hut, the heavy clips started banging against my balls. I shifted the clips to my back pocket, then waited for orders with the others.

Master Chief Pruitt pulled up in a jeep, jumped out and said, "All right, you guys, we've got reports we're gonna get hit. Hard! There's a regiment of NVA's out there gettin' ready to chew you guys a new asshole. We're gonna cut 'em down at the perimeter. Let's go." He turned around and began jogging toward the edge of the base.

I thought the scenario sounded far-fetched. This was not the DMZ. Why would an entire regiment of the North Vietnamese Army infiltrate this close, sneaking around Marine and ARVN (Army of the Republic of Vietnam) installations just to attack a lowly Seabee battalion?

We started a slow jog across the sand between the huts then up the main road toward the base perimeter. The perimeter was marked by coils of barbed wire on top of walls of sandbags, which connected the guard posts. Each post had an M-60 machine gun and was manned by two Seabees from the security platoon. As we ran, sand sucked at my boots and soon I was out of breath. Suddenly I heard a loud explosion. I looked to my right and saw a huge red and black fireball tear through the night sky and billow over a stretch of open land outside the perimeter. A spurt of adrenaline shot through me and I raced toward the edge of the base.

When we got there, we waited. The fireball was gone and the only light came from a half-moon. Since Pruitt was bringing up the rear, we had time to catch our breaths.

"OK," he gasped when he caught up.

He pointed to the sand in front of us. "Two rows."

We straggled forward and separated into two ranks.

"No, down . . . prone . . . get your asses down," he said, gulping for air.

We got down on our bellies in the cool sand.

"Spread out goddammit, spread out. Lock and load," he sputtered.

We spread out. I was in the second row. I reached around behind me and pulled a clip of ammo from my pants pocket. I popped the clip in my rifle, made sure my safety was on and checked out my field of fire.

Someone's head was in my way. My bulky flack jacket bunched up behind my neck and pushed my heavy steel helmet over my eyes. I moved to the side, pulled on the bottom of the jacket to straighten it out and adjusted my helmet so it rested on top of my glasses. I rechecked my field of fire. Now, at least I had a clear shot at the perimeter. Everyone was quiet and waiting. I'd always wondered if I could kill a man. I knew now that it would be easy.

Soon the adrenaline rush wore off. Fifteen minutes and still no sign of the enemy. I wondered if sappers were crawling through the sand, taking their time. Maybe they would slither under the barbed wire and cut the guards' throats. We waited. I began to think about the enemy. Was he a dedicated communist or just a reluctant enlistee like myself? Did it really matter? Regardless of what he believed, I would still have to kill him.

As the ocean breeze cooled us down, I shivered in my sweat-soaked fatigues. Please, let's get this over. Please, let something make sense for a change. Slowly it dawned on me that we'd been had. There would be no attack. I took off my flack jacket and wrapped it around my arms for warmth. Other Seabees were dozing. Even Pruitt was snoring. Just before dawn, the emergency was officially canceled and we went back to our huts to grab a few more winks before morning.

We were never officially told what went wrong. I heard that military intelligence had received reports of thousands of North Vietnamese regulars in the surrounding mountains poised for an attack. When their artillery opened fire, they were supposed to advance. Intelligence decided to set off a barrel of explosives just outside our base to fool them into attacking. We could then cut them down with a wall of fire. But military intelligence got it wrong. The only casualty we sustained was a sprained ankle when someone tripped over a wooden walkway.

21
TAIWAN
September 1968

ABOUT MIDWAY THROUGH the deployment, I took another R&R, this time to Taipei, Taiwan. I wanted a chance to make up for Singapore. I promised myself I'd take my time and choose a woman I felt comfortable with. I would try not to drink too much and we would get acquainted before I took her to my room.

When we arrived at the airport in Taipei, we got the usual speech about staying out of trouble and were asked to turn in any weapons. The orientation officer gave us a small guidebook titled *Thirty Bars in Taipei*. On the cover were two young Chinese women, smiling and dressed in red military-looking tunics. They wore furry ornate headdresses and stood in front of a cable car with mountains in the background. The first page stated,

> *Taipei city has thirty bars approved by the government. We are sure that you, from there, will drink nice wine, enjoy good music, and, of course, get a special service from charming girls. For your personal health, those*

girls are given a periodic physical checkup every two weeks. We wish you have a wonderful time during your short vacation in Taipei. Be sure not to take those girls who are not belong to the bars, because it is not only easy to got trouble but also may suffer from disease.

Thanks for the warning, I thought. Now I feel better. After perusing the book, I climbed into a cab and headed for my hotel. The cab driver carried my suitcase to my room and waited as I changed into my civvies.

"Hurry, Hurry. I get you beautiful girls," he promised.

Then it was back into the cab and to the bars.

He took me to the Pei Ping Bar, a small night spot with a pink neon sign sandwiched between two tall buildings. I paid him and went inside.

The place was cool and dark. I sat down and ordered a 7&7. When I looked up I saw a huge mirror with the reflection of a dozen beautiful women sitting on stools behind me. Some were chatting while others stared into the mirror. Were they staring at me? I chugged down my drink and ordered another one. Easy with the booze, I reminded myself. No need to hurry. Obtaining a sexual partner couldn't have been easier. All I had to do was spin around in my chair and point. Yet, I didn't want to rush things. I tried to mellow out, but the gaze of their eyes on the back of my head made me uncomfortable. In a few minutes I began to feel a soft glow come over me as the alcohol began to do its job. That's better, I thought.

Slowly I swiveled around and found myself face to face with a dozen Chinese whores. I let my eyes wander among their faces. The light was bad and they all wore heavy makeup. I was looking for a girl who would be warm and understanding.

I pointed to one in a yellow sweater. Her hair was tied in a ponytail and she reminded me of a high school cheerleader. Instead, the girl next to her smiled and came over. She was cute too with her white mini-skirt and golden earrings. We talked in broken English and she said her name was Jenny. She took me upstairs to a room with small booths where a waiter brought more drinks. She ordered three drinks to my one, and I was getting charged for them. When the waiter came back with another drink, I pushed it away and paid the bill.

"Let's get outta here," I said. We got up.

"You want me be your girlfriend?"

"Sure. How much?"

"You talk to bar," she said.

Oh shit! Not this again. We went downstairs, and I asked the bartender what the charge was. He reached under the bar, took out a form, and began writing.

"Hold on," I protested. "I just wanna take her out of the bar. I don't wanna marry her."

"You want girl, you sign here," said the skinny bartender. "You pay me 600 NT." (About $15.)

He handed me the form. The words "Contract for Outgoing Waitress" were printed across the top. Below was a list: Movies, Dancing, Sightseeing, Dinner and Other Activities. At the bottom was a provision for "Business Losses." If we didn't get along, I could return her within two hours and get 400 NT back.

I stared at the form.

"You want girl, you sign. Give me 600 NT," the bartender insisted.

I gave him the money, signed the contract, and kept the pink copy.

We took a cab to dinner and then went shopping. Jenny was very attentive and scolded the cab driver when he tried to overcharge me. She exuded a cold confidence. That night was another disastrous episode in bed. Jenny was no better for me than Jeannie. The similarity of their names and the experience led me to believe that fate was having a little joke at my expense.

The next day we rented a boat and went rowing on a lake in the mountains. Jenny insisted on rowing while I took pictures. We visited a Buddhist Temple in the mountains and attended a parade for Ten-Ten Day, October 10, Nationalist China's Independence Day.

My last night with Jenny, I drank heavily. We were in my room with another couple when I was seized by a sense of the absurd and started laughing maniacally. Then, suddenly, I was struck by the tragedy of my situation and started crying. The girls fled while a fellow Seabee tried to comfort me.

I passed out several times in the bus on the way to the plane. When I awoke, we were airborne. I had a cottonball mouth and was sick to my stomach. We landed in Da Nang. From there I got a ride on a C-130 cargo plane to Chu Lai. We sat on webbed seats facing the center of the fuselage. Across from me was a pretty Vietnamese woman with unusually large feet. I thought she might be a male Vietcong soldier in drag. Next to her was a young GI with a dog. As the plane came in for a landing, the dog pissed all over the kid's leg. The Vietnamese woman laughed. I threw up.

22
A Close Call
October 1968

AFTER A COUPLE OF DAYS I recovered from my rest and began counting down my last four months in Vietnam. The weather began to cool off and the twelve-hour work days seemed a little more tolerable.

The monsoon rains hit in the fall. There was no harvest moon, no frost on the pumpkin and no long formations of geese flying south. There was only a bone-chilling dampness and torrents of rain, which turned our supply yard into a mud pit. In the center of the supply yard was a large pile of rotting crates containing the Pre-Positioned Camp Components (PPCC).

The annual supply inspection was coming up, and Master Chief Pruitt wanted us to inventory the PPCC's. When we tried to move them inside with forklifts many of the crates crumbled and fell into the mud. That meant we had to slosh around in the quagmire and pile the contents of the crates onto wooden pallets. After we brought them inside, most of the metal supplies like camp stoves and shovels were rusted, so we threw them away. When we ran out of room, Pruitt persuaded the Seabees to build a special warehouse for the PPCC's. We reordered more supplies and carpenters constructed new storage boxes. Soon we had clean, dry rows of plywood boxes filled with supplies resting on cement floors under an aluminum roof. While we were trying to figure out how to deal with all of our supplies, the Vietnamese had to deal with the lack of them.

One day after dinner, I was sitting on the porch of our hut with Mike Breneman, a burly storekeeper who worked with me at the warehouse. Mike was a well-educated, funny guy who had an overabundance of hair on his body. The Vietnamese girls who helped us around the warehouse teased Mike about it. Playing along, Mike would take off his shirt and chase them around the supply yard like a monkey. The girls would run away laughing, point at him and yell, "Khi, khi, khi," the Vietnamese word for monkey.

In the distance an old beat-up civilian dump truck was heading for the chow hall. The truck belonged to a local family the battalion had contracted with for scavenger services. As the truck got closer I saw that a man was driving with two women sitting next to him. When it reached the chow hall the truck stopped and backed up to a row of garbage cans on a cement slab. Everyone got out. One of the women was young and pretty, wearing high heels, black satin pants and a flowing yellow tunic. The other woman was older and barefoot. The man pulled a garbage can out of the row and opened the lid. It was filled with the uneaten creamed corn from dinner. The young woman rolled up her sleeves, reached into the can up to her elbows and moved her arms around like she was searching for something. She quickly found it — a fully cooked T-bone steak. The three of them gathered around the steak, talking in soothing tones, wiping off the excess corn and stroking the meat like it was a newborn baby. The old woman carefully wrapped the meat in a napkin and put it in a cardboard box on the ground.

I clenched my teeth and grimaced slightly. I had an uncomfortable sense that somehow we were the cause of their poverty.

"Man, they must be starving to death," I said.

Mike leaned forward in his chair and stared at the garbage can. "I'd say they're skimmin' off the high side of our dinner."

"Yeah, but would you eat out of a garbage can if you weren't starving?" I asked.

"It doesn't matter what I'd do."

"Well, I feel a little guilty sitting here with a full belly when they've got to live off our garbage."

"They're lucky we're here. Hell, they probably competed for the refuse contract," Mike said.

"Maybe if we weren't here, there wouldn't be any war and they could raise their own livestock."

"Maybe if we weren't here, the Vietcong would chop off their freakin' heads and stick them on a pole in the middle of the village," said Mike, raising his voice a little.

I sighed. "Who knows?"

The family spent a half-hour with the garbage, extricating choice strips of meat only a couple hours off the grill. When the sun was almost down and the lights of the base flickered on, they climbed aboard the truck and drove away.

☯

I wanted to help the Vietnamese. The battles in the countryside had destroyed many villages and left thousands of children homeless. Many of them roamed throughout the country in bands, stealing what they needed to survive. Some were taken in by orphanages. I visited several orphanages. For a donation of $60, we could clothe and feed one child from an orphanage for a year. Mike Breneman and I decided to sponsor two children from a Protestant orphanage. We were matched up with up with two little girls.

On our Sunday afternoon off we drove to the orphanage to meet them. Mine was an eight-year old named Tich. Her bangs hung down to the tops of her eyelids. She was very quiet and showed little emotion. I knew nothing about her former family or how long she had been in the orphanage. We had a group picture taken then drove to the base for cartoons and cake. At the PX, Mike and I had bought them two lifelike Vietnamese dolls that were clothed in beautiful satin dresses. When they saw the dolls they gasped and smiled. They took off the dolls' hats and ran their fingers through the dolls' hair. They stood them up next to each other and gave them voices. Their joy made me feel good.

After the cartoons, we gave them a tour of our base and then headed back to the orphanage. Tich sat next to me in the bus holding her doll in both hands. About halfway there she slowly reached over and put her little hand on mine. A feeling of warmth rushed through my body. Never had I been so moved by a human touch. I looked at her and smiled. She looked out the window. When we got back to the orphanage I said, "Chou, co," (good-bye to a child).

She looked up at me, bowed a little, and said "Chou an," (good-bye to a young man).

The last time I saw Tich was after Christmas. We had lots of leftover candy and decided to share it with the kids. Mike and I drove to the orphanage and asked Mr. Thao, the director, if we could give them the candy.

Mr. Thao, a middle-aged man who was dressed formally in a suit and tie, spoke no English, so he held up his index finger indicating that we should wait for just a minute. He returned with an interpreter, a teenaged boy. We bowed in greeting.

I asked if we could share our Christmas candy with the children.

The interpreter translated my request and Mr. Thao smiled broadly.

"Mr. Thao thanks you for your generosity and would be delighted to have you share your gifts with the children," said the young interpreter.

"It is we who should be thanking you for giving us the honor of sharing gifts with these beautiful children," I said.

The young man passed this on and Mr. Thao smiled at us. He bowed, went inside, and brought out a long book.

"Mr. Thao would like you to sign this guest book," said the interpreter handing it to me.

I wrote that I wished the war would end soon and thanked them again for allowing us to help the children. After Mike and I signed the book, Mr. Thao walked to the corner of the porch and began ringing a bell.

In a matter of seconds a hundred kids descended upon us.

Mr. Thao held out his arms, indicating they should line up in three rows.

In less than a minute they were all lined up and waiting. We quickly did some math, then handed each child three pieces of candy. After receiving the candy, each child placed their palms together, brought the tips of their fingers to their nose and bowed. When I placed the candy in Tich's hands she looked up at me, smiled and bowed. I wanted to pick her up and give her a hug, but thought better of it. She would have been a wonderful daughter if her parents had lived.

The closest I ever came to becoming a casualty of war happened shortly before we were to leave. One day while I was closing the warehouse before lunch, I heard the long rising and falling whine of the mortar alert siren. As I pulled the two huge, metal-tracked warehouse doors shut, I heard an explosion in the distance. I figured it was probably the Marine air base getting hit again. Their base was a favorite target of the Viet Cong. The mortars usually didn't damage any buildings; they just tore up the airfield, which was constructed of easily replaceable strips of steel matting. As I tried to line up the doors so I could slip the padlock through the holes, I heard another round hit. Closer this time. I stopped and listened. The sirens continued to wail. The warehouse blocked my view of the other bases, so I couldn't see any smoke. Was the enemy walking the rockets in toward a target or were these just random hits? The third explosion was even closer and rattled the doors. I forgot about the lock and started jogging toward the nearest mortar pit, about a quarter-mile away.

In the distance I heard a high-pitched whistling noise. My brain knew I couldn't outrun a rocket, but the rest of my body decided to try. I got a spurt of adrenaline and sprinted toward the pit. The whistling grew louder. I rounded a corner near the huts when a loud "whack" split the air followed by a bone shaking "thud." My momentum kept me upright. I dove into the nearest mortar pit and drew my knees up to my chest. The only thing I could hear was the sound of my heart thumping wildly. I waited for another round to hit, but there was only silence. I would live.

The next day the security platoon picked up several pieces of rocket shrapnel inside our base. The rocket had struck just outside the perimeter. I wondered what it would be like to be under bombardment for hours like the grunts fighting in Dong Ha, near the DMZ! It must be maddening. I gained a new appreciation for their sacrifice and was glad I'd joined the Navy.

The last few months of our deployment passed quickly and soon we were all "short timers" again. We began living in the future. The Vietnam we had been forced to adapt to now began to feel like another planet. We were going back home to "the world" as we called it. The world of the twentieth century with air-conditioned shopping malls and McDonald's restaurants — a world of paved streets and round-eyed women. Yet, in a sense, we could never return to the world as we had known it.

A hint of this new world came in the summer of '68 in a letter from Goerke, my fellow storekeeper who had been discharged after our first deployment and was living in New York City. His letter described a riot at the Democratic National Convention in Chicago where police beat demonstrators and set dogs upon them. Though I'd read about the convention in the military newspaper, *The Stars and Stripes*, I had the impression that the demonstrators were nothing more than an isolated band of troublemakers.

In his letter, Goerke kept referring to the police as "pigs." I had never heard them called that before. It seemed very disrespectful. By his graphic accounts, I assumed he was there, but found out later he had only watched the scenes on TV, shocking scenes that galvanized the anti-war movement.

When I left America, there had been a small, but growing anti-war movement. I returned to a nation that was split between hawks and doves, hippies and straights, radicals and conservatives, parents and children, the young and the old.

23
THE DOORS IN CONCERT
Miami – March 1969

WHEN I RETURNED to Gulfport in February of 1969, I still had a year-and-a-half left on my four-year enlistment. I took two weeks leave and went to Miami even though my parents were still living in Indiana. I wanted to get together with Reilly, an old buddy from North Miami and visit my parents on the way back. Reilly and I had been friends ever since the fifth grade at North Miami Elementary School. Instead of being drafted, he got a medical deferment due to a slight heart murmur. The condition did nothing to slow him down. He worked elevator construction and prepared for his dream trip around the world. While I was in Vietnam, he sent me postcards from the Swiss Alps. It didn't seem fair.

When I met him at the airport, his brown curly hair was hanging down to his shoulders and he had put on some weight, mostly muscle. We drove to his parent's house. They were still living in the old neighborhood on 145th Street. His stepfather was a big guy with a heavy beard who put in elevators for Otis and had gotten Reilly high-paying jobs as a helper. His mother was a cheerful woman who greeted me warmly.

After we got settled, Reilly said he had tickets for us to see The Doors. I didn't know much about the group, but was curious to see what had happened with the music since I'd been gone. We spent a couple days going to the beach and catching up on old times.

The night of March 1 we set out for the Doors concert. On the way, Reilly stopped at his friend's house and bought a bag of marijuana. I had never smoked marijuana, but was ready to give it a try.

When he returned, he had a plastic bag filled with what looked like a pile of lawn clippings.

"Well, Chamberlin, prepare to get high," he said.

"How are we going to smoke this stuff?" I asked.

"I'll roll one on the way to the concert," he said. "You drive."

We changed places and headed toward the expressway.

Reilly took a thin rectangular piece of paper from a flat box, folded the paper in half and began sprinkling the marijuana over it. I tried to watch what he was doing from the corner of my eye, but the light was bad. He managed to roll the paper into a cylinder and I saw him lick it together, then put it in his mouth. When he went to light it, a large flame shot up and he threw the cigarette on the floor.

"Shit, man," he said stomping on it.

"What happened?" I yelled.

"I guess I didn't roll it tight enough."

"Do you want me to pull over?"

"No. Just keep driving. I'll try again."

He salvaged the unburned marijuana from the floor and rolled it with new paper, moistened the ends, and twisted them tight.

When he lit the cigarette again the paper burned about a quarter of the way down and a plume of acrid smoke enveloped the front seat.

Reilly took a long puff and handed it to me.

I dropped the cigarette and swerved as I desperately tried to brush it off my lap.

"Shit, Chamberlin! Are you trying to get us killed?" Reilly shouted.

I pulled over and got out of the car.

"You drive."

After we changed positions Reilly rescued the skinny cigarette that was smoldering near the brake pedal.

"Here," he said, handing it to me.

I carefully placed it between my thumb and index finger, brought it to my mouth and inhaled. It tickled my throat and I coughed a little. I tried again, this time taking a shorter puff.

"Chamberlin, you gotta hold it in for as long as you can," said Reilly.

I inhaled deeply and held it in until I thought my head was going to explode, then exhaled and broke into a massive coughing spasm.

"How does that feel?" Reilly laughed.

"Like I'm about to pass out," I gasped. I was dizzy and disoriented, but got my breath back and handed the cigarette to Reilly.

We passed it back and forth until it was almost gone. When we got down to the end, Reilly put it in his mouth and swallowed it. By the time we arrived at the concert, I was feeling very light- headed. We parked, got out of the car and walked up a long grass berm toward the auditorium. I felt like I was floating.

Inside the auditorium, the seats had been removed and everybody was sitting on the floor waiting for the Doors to appear.

We stepped between bodies and got as close to the stage as we could. I sat next to a girl who was barefoot. She sat in a puddle of Coke, and her feet made dirty swirls in the middle of the floor. I wasn't sure what to expect, but I soon found myself transfixed by the lines on the palm of my hand. They looked like gashes that changed shape and then returned to normal. After a while my high began to wear off. I became aware of the stage. Where the hell was this group anyway? Finally, the Doors came on. Jim Morrison and the other musicians wandered around the stage for a few minutes looking for their instruments. They looked confused. When they finally located them, the guitarists slung their instruments over their shoulders and plugged them in. Suddenly my ears were assaulted by ripping dissonant chords and the random bashing of drums and cymbals. Morrison staggered forward, put both his hands around the microphone and stared at the audience.

"Play *Fire*," someone yelled.

Morrison grinned. "What do you really want to hear?"

"*Fire, Fire*," shouted others in the crowd. The microphones began to screech and Morrison looked back at his band. They tried to play something, but couldn't.

Morrison turned back to the crowd. "No, you don't really want to hear *Fire*. What do you fucking pukes really want?"

By now people were shouting names of songs and obscenities.

"I know what you really want," Morrison shouted, swaggering drunkenly around the mike. "You really want to see my cock."

He unzipped his fly. I couldn't see whether he was actually exposing himself or just teasing the audience.

Everyone was jumping up. "What's he doing, what's he doing?" a girl next to me asked. Suddenly the lights came on and cops dragged Morrison and his band off the stage. The "concert" was over.

The incident was covered widely by the press and Miami churches held a "Youth for Decency" rally in the Orange Bowl Stadium. I had wanted to experience the new hippie subculture, but now I felt ripped off. I came to hear some music, but all I got was a drunk trying to show the audience his wanger.

24
TRIPPING IN NORFOLK
Spring 1970

I BOUGHT A VOLKSWAGEN Karmann-Ghia when I returned to Gulfport and found an apartment with two other Seabees in Pass Christian, a small coastal community about fifteen miles west of Gulfport. I spent my off-hours getting stoned and listening to acid-rock music with my new neighbors, a hippie couple from California.

My new duty station was the USS Orion, home-ported in Norfolk, Virginia where I would spend my last eighteen months in the Navy. The Orion was a large surface ship called a submarine tender that stayed tied to the pier most of the time. It provided supplies for nuclear-powered attack submarines as they came off patrol in the North Atlantic.

I drove to Norfolk and reported to the Orion late in the day. After getting checked in, I was assigned to an upper bunk. It looked cramped. I climbed to the top berth, wedged myself into the cot and stared up at metal rivets inches from my face. Suddenly I became claustrophobic, climbed back down and got a motel for the night.

The next day I met another storekeeper who was looking for a roommate. His name was Jim Foley and he was from

Milwaukee, Wisconsin. Jim was a big man with a light complexion and deep brown, slicked-back hair. He wore thick glasses and had a good sense of humor. He had been a student anti-war activist at the University of Wisconsin who joined the Navy for the same reason I did — to make it through the war. The Orion was his first duty station. We quickly became friends.

Compared with being in Vietnam, duty in Norfolk was almost like being a civilian. The Orion's captain was very liberal and honored the long naval tradition of sailors having beards; soon The Orion became known as "the hippie ship."

On long weekends I could drive to Washington, D.C. for an anti-war demonstration or up to New York City to visit my sister Bette, who was starting a dancing career with the American Ballet Theater. One weekend we saw the Broadway production of *Hair*. Another weekend I drove to Macon, Georgia for a rock festival.

One of my favorite weekends was when two women from Madison, college friends of Jim's, came down for a visit. I hit it off right away with one of them. She was tall with long, sexy legs and auburn hair. That weekend we all jammed into my tiny Karmann-Ghia and drove north to Colonial Williamsburg, a living replica of life in the 1700's. We walked hand in hand through the cobblestone streets and shared molasses cookies in the old bakery. That night, back in Norfolk, we shared my bed and my years of sexual frustration and self-doubt finally came to an end. In too short a time the weekend was over, and the girls returned to Madison. We exchanged letters for a while but eventually she found a boyfriend and stopped writing.

On May 4, 1970, the National Guard opened fire on students who were protesting the war at Kent State College in Ohio and four of them were killed. It was one thing for soldiers to be killed. However, when parents saw their kids being gunned down at an anti-war demonstration, the protest movement ratcheted up a notch.

Two days later riots broke out on campuses all over the country. On May 9, Jim and I drove to Washington D.C. to rally with 100,000 others against the war and the killings at Kent State. I had never seen so many people gathered to protest and felt proud that I was now part of the anti-war movement.

Shortly after we got back to Norfolk, Jim and I saw the movie *Easy Rider*. In the film, Captain America and Billy take LSD and end up with two prostitutes in a cemetery in New Orleans during Mardi Gras. The movie appealed to me because they were on the road and free while I felt like an indentured servant.

I'm not sure whether I decided to take acid to "get my head straight" as the saying went, or do it as a political act of protest. It was probably a combination of the two.

A week later we decided to find some acid and drove to the apartment of a crewmate who told us where we could get some. We brought a short and stocky woman named Karen along with us, whom I had recently befriended at a laundromat. She graciously volunteered to "baby-sit" us. From the apartment, we drove to nearby Virginia Beach and bought two sugar cubes laced with LSD from a hippie sailor out on a jetty.

On the way back to our apartment, Karen drove and Jim was in the back seat. I sat in front and peeled the tinfoil off the cube. It was white and slightly rectangular, with a gray spot and looked harmless. However, I wasn't sure exactly what was inside of it. What if it was poison? There was no way of knowing.

Jim was reluctant to take his acid until he saw what would happen to me, so I put the sugar cube into my mouth and slowly let it dissolve. When we got home I sat on the couch in the living room and waited for the fireworks to begin. Jim and Karen were in the kitchen fixing dinner. I checked my watch. It had been forty-five minutes since I'd taken the acid. I didn't see any little purple men crawling up my leg. No weird voices spoke to me. I stared at the wall for a while, then my salivary glands begin to tingle. A jolt of adrenaline rushed through my body. My heartbeat quickened and blood roared through my eardrums. I took a deep breath, exhaled slowly, and tried to keep calm. Soon I noticed a pink halo around everything.

"Hey you guys, I think it's hitting," I yelled into the kitchen. There was no response.

I checked my watch. It was ten after six in the evening. I got up and walked into the kitchen. A couple days earlier, I had given a cook from a submarine some marijuana in exchange for a large hunk of steak. Now Karen was standing by the stove frying the meat. It looked overdone, but I wasn't sure.

"That's my meat," I growled.

She looked up. "Yes, that's your meat."

"Well, is it done?" I asked.

"I think so," she said.

I reached down, picked the meat off the pan, and ripped off a hunk with my teeth.

I threw it back into the pan. Shit, I thought. It was almost raw. Or was it? It looked like it was just braised on the outside. I picked it up again, tore off a hunk of fat and threw it at Jim, who was sitting in the living room. I hit him squarely in the head.

"What the fuck are you doing, Chamberlin?"

"This shit is raw," I roared.

Karen took the meat from my hand and patiently put it back in the pan. "Dinner will be ready pretty soon," she said, enunciating each syllable very carefully.

Soon dinner was ready. As I stumbled into the dining room, I lost my balance and grabbed the edge of the wall to steady myself, but that didn't help. The wall was wobbling around like a square of Jell-O.

"Holy shit, whaaaaaaaaaa. . . ." I had suddenly lost the power of speech.

I let go of the wall and headed for a chair at the table. What to do now? Sit down? I felt a little guilty about making such a scene with the meat. Maybe I should wait until someone else sat down to see if it was the right thing to do. But now there was the geometrical problem of the table itself, changing from a square to a rectangle and then into a trapezoid, sloping downhill, then uphill. I didn't even know if it was safe to sit down.

"Have a seat," said Karen. Sure, that was easy for her to say. I managed to lower myself into the nearest chair.

Now another problem presented itself. A plate was in front of me with silverware on both sides and an empty glass to the right. Karen even put on a tablecloth. Are they trying to mess with my mind? I suspected they were. The fact that they put on a formal setting while I was on heavy drugs was a clear indication of that. I had a vague impression that Jim was sitting next to me, but I was too intimidated to look up.

Karen came around to my right with a pan and put some niblets of corn on my plate. I stared at the golden yellow pile of pulsating nuggets then grabbed a handful of them.

"Jesus, Chamberlin," Jim said scornfully, "Can't you use a fork?"

I paid him no mind.

After inspecting the nuggets closely and determining they were safe to eat, I licked some of them into my mouth, and embedded the others in my beard. Next, I spread the corn on my plate and started giggling. This was fun. Soon, however, I lost all interest in food.

The room seemed stuffy, so I decided to go outside, but Jim stopped me. What was the problem? Were they taking me prisoner? He led me back to the couch. I started to sweat.

The digital clock in front of me read 7:02. I stared at it, waiting for time to pass. It didn't. After what seemed like half an hour the "2" changed to a "3." I waited for the next change. Nothing. Maybe it was stuck. I tried to get up to examine it, but I couldn't move. The sweat rolled off my brow into my eyes. Finally it became 7:04. Thank God! At this pace I'd never make it to morning.

I wanted this trip to be over. I felt like I was losing my mind. My body grew heavy and I fell to the floor. I felt my body begin to melt into the rug. Soon I no longer existed.

"Everything is oneness," I said to no one in particular.

"Sure, sure," said Jim.

"No, really," I protested. So this is what the mystics were talking about. This must be reality. The barrier between subject and object is just a construct of the ego. We were actually all one entity. My mind drifted in space for a while, then I forgot my name. Was I a human being or a chair? I couldn't go through life like this. Oh, God, I thought. Please give me back my ego.

Gradually the world came back into focus. The room looked familiar. There was furniture in the room. My name was Richard Chamberlin. I saw myself as a separate entity, took a deep breath and smiled.

Jim and Karen were gone. I wondered why they left? In the distance I thought I heard a two-way radio. Suddenly it hit me! They had called the cops. They betrayed me. Why not? I was totally out of control and they freaked out. I started to sweat again. What could I do? Was this really happening? I decided to let the cops come in and arrest me. I'd had a glimpse of the world beyond this widely shared illusion we call reality. They couldn't take that away from me. Besides, Jim and Karen were equally guilty — especially Jim. He and I had bought the acid together. He was an accomplice. I lay there waiting for the bust to come down, but nothing happened.

Soon I became aware of faint voices coming from the upstairs bedroom. Ah! What an idiot I was! I should have known. Jim had taken Karen upstairs and they probably were screwing.

I climbed the stairs. Jim was lying in bed in his underwear and looked very pale. Karen was sitting in a chair next to him.

"Where am I?" asked Jim.

"You're at home in your bedroom," I answered.

"What's my name?"

"Jim Foley," I said. He looked relieved.

"Where were we earlier?" he asked.

"We were at the beach, and before that we were at John Foley's house," I answered as truthfully as I could.

The look of relief vanished, and a crazed, suspicious look filled his eyes.

"What's my name?" he began again.

"Jim Foley."

"Then who is John Foley?" he asked, with a note of panic in his voice.

"You are Jim Foley, "I said. "Jim, not John. Your name is Jim. John is the other Foley. We were at his house earlier. He's a storekeeper, too, but you are not John. You are Jim." He looked confused.

We went on like that for about an hour, until the acid began to wear off. Jim finally regained his sense of identity and I went back to my bedroom. I tried to sleep, but I couldn't. When I closed my eyes, extremely vivid images from the beach began flashing through my head — white-capped waves breaking on the beach, brown sand castles, snazzy surfboards, the old wooden pier, flocks of hovering seagulls and bronzed girls in bikinis.

After a few days, I began to feel normal again. I could fall to sleep without flashing on images. I stopped seeing a pink halo around everything. Yet, something had changed. Images had new meanings and thoughts connected in different ways. An advertisement for a new Buick in a magazine struck me as especially troubling. An older elegantly dressed couple stood smugly in front of the car. The ad copy asked, "Now wouldn't you really rather have a Buick?" I thought about the ad. Something didn't seem right. Then it hit me. Rich people would rather not hear about all the riots, the atrocities, the killings, and the bombings. They wanted to ignore the worlds' suffering and indulge their appetites for material pleasures. It distressed me that in spite of all the government lying, corporate profiteering, lynching, and racism, GM's customers would "really rather have a Buick."

I became obsessed with the ad, cut it out and pasted it in the center of a collage surrounded by pictures of mangled GI's, anti-war protesters, Bobby Kennedy laying in a pool of blood, Hewey Newton and the Black Panthers hoisting shotguns, and Janis Joplin screaming into a microphone. I framed the collage and proudly displayed it on the wall.

One day Jim brought home an underground comic book called *Mother's Oats*. The first story was called "The Doings of Dealer McDope," by Dave Sheridan. In the comic, Dealer McDope, disguised as an old woman, comes home after a hard day selling drugs. He takes off his mask and overcoat and sits down in his favorite chair to relax when suddenly a rectangular hole appears right in front of him. "Hey . . . Fa-Fa-a-a-r fucking out!" he says. "There's a fuckin' hole in my reality." He grabs his water pipe, jumps into the hole and is transported to the city of Long Toe Shoe, "a place of wonder beyond the woods of bad news," where he meets Petipoo, keeper of the talking mushrooms. Together they journey to meet the King who is a connoisseur of mind-expanding drugs. McDope ingests a mushroom from the King and flies off into the far reaches of the universe screaming "GODZILLA MOTHERFUCKERS!!!!" When he comes down he's in his own apartment. The cops bust in and McDope escapes through an open window.

There was no doubt that after our acid trip there was a hole in our reality, yet it seemed there was also a hole in the reality of society as well. Living in a place where leaders had expanded minds seemed preferable to living in "the woods of bad news" where politicians turned a deaf ear to the reality of human suffering.

Five years later, cruising the speed-blurred freeways of Los Angeles, I was still trying to reconstruct my own reality.

PART FOUR
THE TRIP BACK

25

BACK ON THE ROAD
California Coast – August 1975

A WEEK IN L.A. WITH KELLY was long enough. I was becoming numb with all the signs, cars, crowds, buy this, buy that, eat, spend, consume, do, and talk. The frantic speed of living was wearing me out and Kelly's lifestyle was poisoning my body with junk food. It was time to leave and hitch up the coast to San Francisco then head back east.

Kelly drove me to Ventura, a small, attractive, coastal town sixty miles north of L.A. We had lunch at an outdoor restaurant beneath a magnificent oak and then he dropped me off on the coastal highway. On my own for the first time in a week, I felt vulnerable and abandoned. I'd been safe for too long. I had to get back into the rhythm of the road.

I walked around a bend in the road and saw another hitchhiker with curly red hair wearing a floppy sombrero and tire-tread Mexican peasant sandals.

"How ya doin'?" I called out.

"I dunno," he answered. "Just got here myself."

"I'm tryin' ta make it to Berkeley sometime," I said, as I got closer.

"Yeah, me too."

He wore silver reflective sunglasses so I couldn't see his eyes, but he seemed friendly enough.

I put out my hand. "Richard."

"Mike." He shook my hand.

"Where ya coming from?"

"Mexico."

"Far out."

"Yeah," he said. "I'm just trying to get back into this scene." He took off his hat and ran his fingers through his hair.

"Yeah, I know. I'm trying to get out of the L.A. scene. It was getting kind of heavy." I stared south toward the smog on the horizon.

"Yeah."

I gazed into the blue haze of the Pacific Ocean as we bantered back a forth, lackadaisically thumbing cars as they drove by.

"Man, this really sucks," said Mike. "Down in Mexico you get a ride right away. They got a car filled with people and they still give you a ride. They've really got heart. Up here, the Norte Americanos . . . Man, everyone thinks you're gonna rip 'em off . . . what shit!"

Finally we got a ride with a married couple who belonged to a Christian commune located up the road. They said we could probably spend the night there.

We arrived at the commune at about six o'clock. It was a disheveled-looking settlement of tin shacks and chicken coops surrounding a burned-out barn and an old farmhouse with peeling white paint.

The couple introduced us to a small, ragged-looking young man they called Peter, who wore a dirty baseball cap. We followed Peter into the farmhouse. Inside was a crude communal kitchen and bunking area. There was a large pan on the stove filled with cold vegetarian gruel and rice.

"It's not much, but it's all we got," said Peter.

We were both very hungry so we each had a bowl full. It tasted bland and formed a gooey mass inside my mouth. I looked around and found some weak Kool Aid to wash it down with. After eating, we went outside to look around. In the distance I noticed a man with long dark hair and a beard standing next to the remains of the barn.

"Who's that?" I asked Peter.

"That's John. He started the commune a couple years ago."

"Is he a minister or something?" I asked.

"Oh no," said Peter. "I don't know exactly what he did before he came here, but he's got the light of Jesus in his eyes. If you're around him long enough you'll see. People come off the road like yourselves and stay because they can feel his power."

"What happened with the barn?" I asked. "Did it get struck by lightening or something?"

"No one knows exactly what happened," said Peter. "Some people say God burned it down."

"Why would God burn it down?" I asked. "I thought this was a Christian commune."

"Let's take a walk," said Peter. Mike and I followed him down a path that led into a pasture.

"I'm probably not supposed to tell you this, but I'm gonna be leaving soon," said Peter in a low tone. "Things are kind of falling apart around here. You got the vegetarians and the meat eaters. Last week John ordered the killing of a pregnant rabbit for meat. The vegetarians objected, but the rabbit was slaughtered anyway and served up in a stew. Shortly after that, the barn burned down. Some thought it was retribution from God. Others thought it was arson."

"What do you think?" asked Mike.

"Could have been both."

"What do you mean?"

"God could have put the idea in someone's head."

I wondered if God was putting thoughts in their heads about us. We walked back to the farmhouse area. Near the barn, two other men with beards had joined John. They were talking and occasionally they glanced up at us.

"Probably wonderin' if we're some new converts, "Mike said.

"I got some bad vibes about this place," I said. "God musta not been too happy about these people." I didn't really believe in God, but pretending to seemed like the appropriate thing to do.

Shortly before dusk, we found out we'd have to sleep outside because there was no room in the house.

"They call themselves Christians, then they make their guests sleep outside," grumbled Mike as we unrolled our sleeping bags on the lawn.

After it got dark, shadowy clusters of people in cloaks began arriving at the house. When everyone was inside, they closed the door.

From where Mike and I were camped out in the side yard, we could only see silhouettes of people through a shade illuminated by candles. The house was quiet for a few minutes and then we heard a barely audible murmur. Other voices joined in, as the murmur became a wail and then a chant.

"What are they doing?" I asked Mike.

"They're prayin'."

Suddenly a woman's voice emerged. It was loud and she spoke in a strange language I'd never heard before.

I looked at Mike. "What kind of language is that?"

"She's speakin' in tongues."

I was skeptical. "Maybe Russian or Hebrew?"

"No. She's speakin' in tongues," whispered Mike. "She's got a spirit inside of her. I seen this before. When they get the spirit, it's like they're in a trance. They just have to do what the spirit tells 'em to do."

Suddenly the image of Charlie Manson flashed into my head. Manson and his cult of drifters ritually killed three people in 1969. The Manson clan lived on a dilapidated ranch in California. But wait, Manson said he was God. These people were Christians. They worship God. I thought of their leader John, standing next to the barn. So what if these people weren't your average Sunday morning Bible thumpers? The first Christians were poor, oppressed wretches living in the desert. Don't let middle-class American paranoia get the best of you, I thought. Still I couldn't get the wild-eyed face of Charlie Manson out of my mind.

The pitch of the woman's voice dropped suddenly, taking on a more authoritative quality and then rose again. Shadows flitted about the shade. There was a scuffling sound followed by the sound of a body hitting the wall.

I looked at Mike. His eyes were wide. He looked back at me.

"Must be an Injun spirit," he said. "The Injuns get mighty pissed about things. I guess I'd get upset about things too if I was an Injun 'cuz all the killin' and rapin' that the white man did to them."

After a while the talking, the wailing and the singing stopped. We heard the low rumbling voices of prayer and then the commune members filed out silently and disappeared into the thick fog. We dozed a little and waited until the fog-shrouded darkness gave way to the luminescent glow of dawn. Then we folded up our sleeping bags and headed for our lifeline to the world — the highway.

When we reached a low spot in the main road the fog thinned a bit, but then grew thickener as we went up the other side. We trudged along the rocky shoulder and put as many hills between the commune and ourselves as we could, listening for the sound of approaching cars, only to be enveloped in a cottony silence. In my sleep-deprived state of mind I imagined a car full of drugged Christian fanatics swirling out of the mist to avenge some unknown slight we had perpetrated against the tribe of John.

Fortunately that didn't happen, but I was soon to immerse myself into an even more bizarre episode, this time of my own making.

26
TRIPPING AT LITTLE SUR
August 1975

SHORTLY AFTER WE LEFT the commune we got a ride in a VW van with some other hitchhikers. The driver was an older man with long gray hair and a beard. He was wearing a crudely tailored deer hide tunic lashed together with rawhide and was headed north to Big Sur. This seemed like the perfect place to take the acid I'd bought back in L.A. I was out in nature, free to expand my consciousness and I was sure I'd have a better trip than I'd had in Norfolk five years earlier. I unzipped a side pocket of my pack and retrieved a hit of blotter acid, a small square of cardboard soaked in LSD. After placing the square on my tongue, I stretched out on the floor of the van and watched the gray sky alternate with patches of fog and low-hanging clouds.

We began a slow climb up a long, steep grade. The fog was so damp that droplets of water began to form on my clothes. By the time we reached the top, I was tripping. Suddenly the man in animal skins stopped to let us off. Why was he pulling over here, I wondered? This wasn't the best place to leave the shelter of a warm van. I gave him a few bucks for gas and he took us down the other side. We descended into Little Sur, just north of the park, where Mike and I parted company. He wished me luck and caught another ride going north.

I stood on the side of the road and stared at the ocean. A few hundred yards off shore there was a jagged prominence partially shrouded in fog. I walked down a steep incline onto a wind-scoured beach. The wind was howling, so I ducked into a low pocket of sand behind a dune where I sat down, crossed my legs and tried to get centered. I didn't want to lose track of my ego this time.

For several minutes I sat there repeating my name to myself. As the acid began to peak, I felt as if the world was crashing around me like a bad heavy metal rock finale. Thousands of wind-borne flecks of sand skimmed over the edge of the pocket and bit into my face. I tilted my straw hat into the wind to block the stinging particles. When I glanced up I noticed the shapes of two people huddled on the lee side of a pile of driftwood about twenty yards in front of me, their arms wrapped around each other. Suddenly I felt totally abandoned. Their intimacy reminded me of my own isolation. I took out my harmonica and began playing Dylan's *Mister Tambourine Man*, over and over again to comfort myself. After a while I got up and peered through the fog off shore. The tall shapes of the giant rocks swayed and twisted in the distance and I felt like I was starting to break though to an alternative reality.

A huge white bird flew toward me, possibly a spirit bird from another world. I called up to it, "Come here my brother." The bird hovered for a moment, then defecated on my hat — perhaps it was a sign. I sat back down and gazed into the fog.

Finally the wind died down, the fog lifted and the world stopped crashing down around me. I got up, slung my pack on my shoulders and walked north along the beach, leaving the couple alone. Offshore, heavy swells were still rolling in. They crested, then broke against the rocks. I walked toward a stream that flowed down from the mountains, its shallow rivulets branching off to form a broad alluvial fan where it met the beach. In the distance, beyond the stream, was a hill. Most of it was overgrown with dense vegetation, but there appeared to be a clear patch of ground that overlooked the beach. I thought it would make a good campsite.

I took off my shoes and waded across the icy water. The cool sensation of water and pebbles on the bottom of my feet helped center me and bring me down from acid trip. When I reached the other side, I put my shoes on and continued walking. As I neared the tree line, I saw smoke from a campfire. Damn it, I thought. I wanted to be alone. When I reached the patch of ground I'd observed from the beach, three teenagers were heating up a pot of water over a fire.

"How ya doin?" I said, smiling from a distance.

A young woman turned to look at me, hesitated a moment and then said, "Hi."

"Sorry to interrupt your camp," I said.

The two others looked up. One was a heavier young woman with long black hair, the other a boy with blond hair and a Grateful Dead tee-shirt.

I approached slowly and tried to act normal.

"I've been hitching up the coast and was looking for a place to spend the night."

"There are some more campsites over there," said the first young woman, pointing to a clump of trees.

"Yeah, I saw them from the beach," I said.

I threw my pack down and took a swig of water from my canteen.

"Do you want some tea?" she said.

"That would be great."

She got a ceramic cup, lifted the pot from the fire and poured me some tea.

"Here," she said, pointing to a large rock outcropping. "Have a seat."

I sat down and she started telling me about their week-long hike through Big Sur country.

Their fire was getting low, so, believing the acid had worn off, I offered to cut some firewood. I got up and grabbed their small camping ax.

The ground was soft and there was no chopping block, so I tried to split a log by standing it on end. The log tipped over each time I got ready to take a whack at it. I decided to steady it with my left hand and let go just before the ax bit into the wood, but my timing was off. Instead, I chopped a huge gash into my thumb. I threw the ax down and grabbed my wrist. Blood began gushing from the wound.

"Holy shit!" I yelled.

I tore off my flannel shirt and wrapped it around my thumb. Now what?

The kids ran over to me.

"Do you want a bandage?" asked the girl.

When I unwrapped my thumb, it started bleeding again. A bandage wouldn't do the trick. I needed stitches.

I tied the shirt around my thumb, said, "Gotta go," then began desperately crashing through the underbrush toward the road where I hoped to get a ride to a hospital.

I was in luck. A car was parked along the shoulder, but I couldn't see who was inside because of the heavily tinted windows. I went over to the driver's side as calmly as possible and knocked on the window. The window rolled down a couple inches and a man peered up at me.

"Excuse me, sir," I said. "I had a little accident over there camping. Seems I chopped my thumb with an ax and I wonder if I could get a ride with you to a hospital." I held up my thumb wrapped in the bloody shirt.

"There's no hospital around here," he said, turning his head from side to side as if he was looking for someone else. I wondered what he was doing parked in the middle of nowhere. Was he expecting someone?

I tried to explain myself. "I was just hitching up the coast . . . on a little vacation and I was camped over there." I pointed to the trees. I was getting desperate.

"Look," I said. "You don't know me, but I'd really appreciate a ride. I can't stop the bleeding."

He rolled the window down a little more. I heard the squeal of a two-way radio and wondered if he was a cop.

"Just a minute, I'll try to get some help on my radio," he said. "Baker one, Baker one. I've got a 10-33. Is anybody listening? Over." All I could hear was a lot of squealing and chopped voices. He tried several more times.

"We're in a bad reception zone," he said. "The mountains block out a lot of it. We were just trying to communicate with some ships off shore."

Ships! That gave me an idea. I reached into a back pocket and took out my wallet.

"Here's my Navy Reserve ID," I said handing him my long-expired red Navy identification card. He turned it over and handed it back.

"You're in luck, pal. There's a Naval Reserve Station just up the beach a couple miles," he said. "Hop in and we'll give you a ride."

"Thanks a lot," I said and got in. There was a pretty young woman with long black hair in the back seat with her arm around another woman whose face I couldn't see. As we pulled out, the other woman glanced over at me. I jumped back. One of her eyeballs bulged out, covered with a gray translucent membrane.

"Uh, how ya doin'?" I said.

The pretty woman nodded. Her eyes were red and her cheeks were wet with tears.

"I'm really sorry to bother you, but I . . . uh . . . I cut my thumb," I said holding up the bloody shirt.

I felt guilty about interrupting their privacy. Maybe the woman with the big eye had terminal cancer and they were comforting her. I didn't know what to say. I winced and turned back to the driver.

"You think they'll patch me up there? I've been out of the Navy for a while."

"I know some people up there," he said.

When we got to a small observatory, he ran inside. A short while later, he returned and said there wasn't a corpsman on duty, so they couldn't treat me. He offered to give me a ride to a hospital in Monterey about 20 miles up the coast.

"Yeah, great, thanks a lot, "I said. I raised my left arm in the air and gripped my wrist to act as a tourniquet. I leaned back in the seat and tried to relax. A half-hour later he dropped me off at the emergency room.

Once inside, a doctor cleaned out the wound, applied a butterfly bandage, and gave me a tetanus shot. I was glad I didn't need stitches. Before I left I gave them a phony address in Los Angeles and told them to bill me there.

I had left my pack with the kids so hitched a ride back to camp, looking forward to relaxing. I returned around sunset, and the kids were still there. By now most of the LSD had worn off and I played my harmonica as they drifted off to sleep. I walked to the edge of the small hilltop overlooking the ocean and unrolled my sleeping bag. I found a rock to sit on and watched as the full moon rose on the dark blue horizon — its white light making the nearby stream sparkle. When my eye lids began to get heavy, I crawled inside my bag and looked up at the stars until I fell asleep.

27
TANGO IN TAHOE
August 1975

MY THUMB WAS THROBBING the next morning, but I bore the pain as penance for my stupidity. Why did I do it? I could have enjoyed the trip without the acid. I could have camped out, met some kids, and reveled in the moonlight without chopping my hand. I made a mental note to lay off the psychedelics.

I hitched up the coast and stopped in Santa Cruz, where I treated myself to a carafe of wine at an outdoor café. I was tired of hitchhiking. Mike had told me about a nude beach in the area called Bonnie Dunes. I asked around and, without much trouble, found out where it was. I decided it would be a nice place to spend a couple days recuperating.

I headed back onto the coastal highway and thumbed down a car with a young couple in it. Coincidentally, they were on their way to the nude beach. After a short drive, we pulled off the road and got out. The beach was at the bottom of a cliff, sheltered from view. I followed them down a steep, dirt path. When we reached the sand at the bottom the beach was empty. The couple continued walking ahead of me and motioned for me to follow. We walked toward a tall rock wall that jutted out into the ocean. As we got closer, I saw a shoulder-high, square tunnel in the wall and followed the couple through it. We came out on a broad expanse of beach shaped like a half-moon encircled by tall sand cliffs.

A few nude sunbathers were scattered around the beach. I dropped my pack in the sand as the couple threw their towels on the beach. The young woman kicked off her sandals, nonchalantly slipped out of her cutoffs, and removed her tee-shirt. She had a slender, bronzed body, unblemished by even a hint of a bathing suit line. Her boyfriend stripped in the same casual manner then they ran out into the surf.

I took off my clothes, rubbed some of their lotion on my body and stretched out a towel. Soon I began to sweat and sat up. The couple came back, greased each other up with oil and took off again, heading for some big boulders at the end of the beach.

I looked around. A solitary woman with a white dress came through the rock tunnel and sat down nearby. She lifted her dress off over her head and placed it next to her on the sand. Her skin was white and pasty and she had flaccid breasts. She sat down and lit a cigarette then wrapped her arms around her knees and stared at the ocean. I looked around. No one else was with her. Here was a naked woman alone on the beach. This was my big chance to make my move. I wondered what to say?

While living in Miami, I'd developed several opening lines for beach situations such as this. One was, "Hi, could you watch my stuff while I go swimming?" That didn't seem right because the water was too cold. Another line was, "Can I borrow some suntan lotion?" But I had plenty of suntan lotion.

While I was running scenarios through my mind, a man with gray hair, wearing jeans and smoking a cigarette, sat down next to her. They started talking then walked off together. Just as well, I thought. I sculpted a little pillow for myself in the sand and lay back .

As the sun got lower, a cool breeze began to blow in from the ocean. The couple came back, donned their clothes and asked me if I wanted a ride out. I decided to stay. Someone started a bonfire. Later I bummed a couple hot dogs and a beer, then began looking for a safe spot to spend the night. I found a place near the rock wall and began digging, but the more sand I scooped out, the wetter it got. Finally, tired of digging in the dark, I curled up in my damp sleeping bag and tried to shiver away the cold.

After grabbing a couple fitful hours of sleep, the cold blackness of night slowly turned into the damp gray chill of dawn. I waited until the sun cleared the rim of the cliff, then crawled out of my sleeping bag. I loaded my pack, then shimmied up the precipice. My thumb was still throbbing as I caught a ride to a truck stop where I gulped down several steaming cups of coffee with lots of cream and sugar. It was time to head home.

I hitched up the coast to San Francisco and decided to take the new Bay Area Rapid Transit (BART) to Berkeley and hitch back east on Interstate 80. The only subways I'd ever ridden were the loud, dirty ones in New York City and Chicago. The BART, by contrast, was sleek and had a gleaming silver-colored interior. We pulled out of the station with a soundless, even acceleration, a welcome change from the clackety subways I was used to. Across the aisle to my right sat a deeply suntanned young woman with silver and gold bracelets and long hoop earrings. She wore a white beach dress, casually unbuttoned at the top. From the side I could see most of her bronzed left breast. I got off the BART in Berkeley and made my way to Telegraph Avenue, the street leading to the interstate highway.

There were several hitchhikers along the road, so I got in line. I waited a while without much luck, then made a sign with my notebook reading "I-80 EAST." After about fifteen minutes of fairly heavy traffic I still couldn't get a ride. I checked my map. Reno was the next big town, so I turned to a new page and wrote "RENO."

The wind was picking up so I held the sign in one hand and kept my hat from blowing off with the other. A tan Volkswagen pulled over to the curb next to me. A woman with mirror sunglasses and short red hair leaned over and cranked down the window.

"Hi," I said. "Goin' to Reno?"

"Oh, you're not Robert," she said.

"No, I'm not," I admitted, "But I sure could use a ride out of here."

"Well, I thought you were a friend of my brother's. He was supposed to be hitching back to Reno today."

"I wish I was the friend of your brother, but I could still use a ride," I said.

"Well . . . okay; just throw your stuff in the back seat."

I threw my pack and sleeping bag into her car and off we went.

This was a rare treat, getting a ride with a single woman. I glanced over at her. She was wearing an Indian print tunic and a necklace of feathers and bones. I couldn't see her eyes because of the sunglasses, but I did notice she had a light complexion and some freckles.

"My name's Richard," I said.

"Nice to meet you." She extended her hand. "I'm Maureen."

"You from Reno?" I asked, shaking her hand.

"I'm just living in Tahoe for the summer."

Living in Lake Tahoe isn't cheap, I thought. Maybe she's rich.

"I'm a waitress," she said, as if reading my mind.

"Far out!" I liked waitresses.

"I'm headed back to Wisconsin. Gonna start school in the fall."

"Oh, yeah? I just graduated from UC Berkeley," she said. "I'm just working for a while 'til I can get into grad school."

"What's your major?"

"Social Work."

Ah, social work, I thought. The academic refuge for dreamers and idealists. The necklace, the tunic and the peasant sandals — it all fit together. She was a soul mate.

When we reached the mountains, she pulled into a little grocery and bought a six-pack of beer. After we got back on the road, she brought out a joint and we got high.

We started up the steep western slope of the Sierras. "What kind of social work are you into?" I asked.

"I don't know," she said. "I was thinking of getting into the hospice movement. I went to a lecture by Kubler-Ross a couple weeks ago."

I was familiar with Kubler-Ross, the Viennese-trained psychotherapist-visionary. She claimed that at the moment of death people experience a feeling of being rushed down a bright tunnel of light and meeting an all-loving being at the end.

"Yeah, I've heard of her," I said slowly. "It sounds like she's made contact with the afterlife, but I don't think western medicine is ready to accept her ideas."

"I know all about that," said Maureen, "but the lecture was about the stages of loss people go through before they die. There's a hospice movement in California and I thought maybe. . . ." Her voice trailed off. "Well, I don't know, I just thought maybe I could get in with them."

Maureen jammed on the brakes, narrowly avoiding a deer that had run in front of us. "Yeah, well, whatever gets you off," I said. I didn't want to talk about death any more. We were here in the beautiful mountains. I wanted to talk about life. The VW engine began to buck as Maureen downshifted.

"I'm into Ram Dass myself," I said changing the subject. "He is more into the present. You know, being here now. He talks about experiencing death as a kind of meditation. I mean like thinking of what it is to die and then coming back and experiencing life anew." Damn it, I thought. Here I was talking about death again.

"What's your sign?" asked Maureen.

"I'm a Capricorn," I said. "I've got my moon in Taurus and my rising sign there, too. I'm a triple earth sign kind of guy. How about you?"

"I'm a Pisces," said Maureen. "Can't you tell?" She smiled, shaking her necklace of feathers and bones.

"Oh, yes. How could I have missed that?" I laughed, throwing up my hands. "A very spiritual sign. You must have great intuition."

"Yes, I do." She smiled and lightly touched my arm. I returned her smile and settled back in my seat, just trying to be here now.

The sun was low on the horizon when we got to Lake Tahoe, a well-timbered mountain resort on the California-Nevada border. I was ready to get out and thank her for the ride, but Maureen asked me if I wanted to go swimming. I said okay.

We drove to her cottage, an A-frame that she shared with two other women who were gone for the week. She loaned me her brother's swimming trunks and, as the sun began to set behind the mountains, we hurried toward a small cobble-stoned beach next to a pier.

We walked to the edge of the pier. I screamed "Geronimooooo!" and dove into the icy mountain lake. When I came up for air, Maureen was beside me in chest-high water. I gave her a hug. We were both shivering and soon we were kissing and groping each other.

We went back to the cottage and made love on her waterbed. After years of being stranded on desolate crossroads, of getting beer cans thrown at me by passing drunks, of getting hassled by the cops and rednecks, of being cold and broke, I figured this was the closest to hitchhiker paradise I would ever get.

The next day Maureen had to work, but promised we would have dinner on the patio when she got home. I went to the beach and propped myself up against a pine tree to watch tourists and read a book from my backpack — *Space, Time and Beyond* by Bob Toben.

Toben wrote that when we go through life we select what essentially are different parts of various universes to construct our own reality that becomes encapsulated in a cone of light. The book suggested that we can escape from the cone of light and see alternative universes through altering our consciousness.

Just then a man driving a large camper pulled into a nearby parking spot and he and his wife got out. Each of them wore shorts and Disneyland tee-shirts. The rest of the family piled out and the two kids went tearing off toward the beach. One of the little girls was encased in a plastic inner tube with a Donald Duck head and the other wore a similar Mickey Mouse tube. They jumped into the water and splashed around. The wife went inside the camper and brought out a Pekinese dog with a pink ribbon. She put the dog on a leash, and it began yapping at nothing in particular. They each put on their sunglasses, popped a beer and began watching TV, as the dog continued barking and a powerboat raced dangerously close to the bathers.

I stretched out on the grass and wondered what would happen if I suddenly was able to step out of my cone of reality. What if Disneyland really existed in another dimension where mice were philosopher kings and talking ducks were like knights enforcing the order of the realm? What if Pekinese dogs with pink ribbons were the guardians of the border between the various worlds and the water of Lake Tahoe was just sloshing in the space between our reality and the next?

When Maureen returned from work that evening, she fixed dinner and we ate on the patio beneath the tall pines. We spent the night together. The next day Maureen was off work, so we visited her sister who lived nearby. We drove part way around the lake to another A-frame cottage, located in a small subdivision.

As I sat there talking with them about business and fishing, I began to feel that I was in the wrong universe. What the hell was I doing here? My place was out on the six-lane interstate, riding along at eighty miles-per-hour, listening to engines hum and tires whine in the cool desolate night. Normality was shooting by towns like these, seeing them as merely clusters of twinkling lights. Their inhabitants' lives were no more important to me than the sagebrush along the highway.

I tried hard to concentrate on what her brother-in-law was saying. Just then, two boys ran into the room, excited to see their Aunt Maureen. The older boy, who looked to be around seven, ran up to Maureen and hugged her. The younger one, a little blond boy, stood and stared at me with big blue eyes. I stared back. For a moment, it felt like I was seeing myself when I was that age.

Suddenly I was filled with a powerful, almost instinctual sense of my own propensity for fatherhood. If Maureen and I somehow got married and had a child, this is what he would look like. I held out my arms, but the boy continued to stare, then turned around and ran back to his dad. I felt rejected.

Later that day we took the children fishing off a pier. The sky was overcast and a cold wind blew down from the mountains, whipping up a white froth on the surface of the lake. I held Maureen close and indulged myself for a moment in the fantasy that we were family and my hitchhiking experience was only the dream of a husband who occasionally let his mind wander.

But slowly, reluctantly, reality seeped back into my consciousness. I remembered the Zen proverb that life is like water. The tighter you try to grasp it, the more it runs through your fingers. I was grasping.

That night Maureen and I made love like there was no tomorrow. She said she would consider going to grad school at the University of Wisconsin, and we promised each other we would write. The next day I rode with her to work and she served me a free breakfast. We said good-bye with a long, passionate embrace behind the restaurant under a huge Douglas Fir.

Two months later Maureen wrote to tell me she was going to school at Stanford. I wrote back and wished her well.

28
THE HONEST THIEF
August 1975

I THREW MY PACK ONTO MY SHOULDERS and hitched a short ride to the interstate. I got another ride to the western outskirts of Reno, Nevada then east with a guy in a pick-up truck. His face was a dark, sun-baked brown and he wore a rumpled hat and wraparound sunglasses.

"How ya doin' son," he said after I got in. "My name's Jack. Here, have a beer." He handed me a can.

I introduced myself, popped the top open and took a swig. It was barely cold and started foaming up in my stomach. I belched. Jack gulped down his beer as if it was water, crushed the can against his leg and threw it out the window.

He reached into the ice chest on the seat between us and took another can that by now was floating in water. As we headed into the desert east of Reno, a dozen hitchhikers were strung out on the shoulder of the road. Some sat while others stood with their thumbs out. Some had suitcases or packs, but most didn't.

"Where'd all those guys come from?" I asked.

"Those are the boys that Lady Luck abandoned, son," said Jack. "I've been there myself once or twice."

"Don't the cops hassle them?" I asked. "I mean they're right out here on the interstate."

"Cops don't hassle 'em because they don' wanna deal with 'em. Whatchya gonna do? Put 'em in jail? They got no money for bail. Pretty soon you got your jail all filled up with a bunch a losers. Then you gotta feed 'em, take 'em to court and listen to 'em bellyache about how they was fucked over by the casino. It just ain't worth it."

Jack talked hard and fast, like something was eating on his nerves. He said between his gambling losses and odd jobs he'd done thirteen years in prison for everything from stealing hubcaps to armed robbery. Recently he'd married a woman whose father had died and left her a big chunk of money. At the moment though, he was upset about the behavior of his two-year-old daughter.

"I love that little kid, but you know what? You know what?" Jack took a heavy hit off his cigarette.

"What?"

"Sometimes I hate her guts." Bang. He hit the steering wheel with the bottom of his palm to drive home the point.

I looked up. Was this guy going to lose it? I couldn't read his face because he was wearing sunglasses.

"Sometimes a man's just gotta get away to straighten out his life," he said.

"See that dog in the back?"

I turned around and looked at the bed of his truck where a brown German Shepherd was curled up in a large ball.

"Yeah," I said slowly.

"I love him too. When he gets old I'm not gonna let him get sick. You know what I'm gonna do?"

"No, what?"

"I'm gonna bury him."

I started to ask him if he was going to kill the dog first, but stopped myself and merely nodded.

"See this truck? I love it. When it gets old I'm not gonna let it fall apart. You know what I'm gonna do?"

By now I thought I knew, but asked anyway. "No, what?"

His hands tightened around the steering wheel and he leaned back locking his arms. He turned toward me. I could feel an intense glare. "I'm gonna bury it, too."

I wondered what would happen if Jack's cute little two-year-old girl came toddling up to him with a question after he'd had too much to drink. No, it was too frightening to think about.

I nodded, afraid that if I said the wrong thing he'd slam on the brakes, grab the shotgun from the rack behind the seat, and blow the back of my head apart as I ran shrieking across the desert.

I tried to relax. Jack was quiet for a few minutes, like he was trying to work out something in his mind. Then he tossed me a plastic baggie of marijuana and some cigarette papers.

"Here," he said. "You know how to roll a joint?"

I rolled one and we passed it back and forth. We popped open a couple more beers and I settled back in the corner between the seat and the door and closed my eyes. The sun was setting and the air was growing cooler. Jack turned on the heater and a warm, cozy feeling overtook me. I decided there could be worse things to do with your life than drive through the desert at sunset with a German Shepherd, a bag of weed, a madman named Jack and his 12-gauge shotgun. I fell asleep, lulled by the hum of the engine and the warm air blowing from the vents.

As we neared a cutoff, Jack woke me up. It was almost dark and we were going down a long grade. The dark blue of the east was eating up the reddish glow of the west. Ahead the lights from Wells, Nevada twinkled like stars in the enormous blackness of the desert.

Before I got out Jack laid a twenty-dollar bill on the seat and told me to take it. I picked it up and thanked him.

"Don't thank me," he said. "I'm just passing it on. I've been hitchin' this desert for a long time and I've been busted without a cent to my name. I know how it is. All I ask is when you see a dude in need, just help him out. I don't care what you do with it; it don't matter none."

29
ERNIE PYLE'S TYPEWRITER
LaPorte, Indiana – 1972-1973

JACK PULLED INTO A TRUCK STOP and I got out. I called Dave Crum in Fort Collins, Colorado from a pay phone and told him I'd be there in a day or two. Dave and I had become friends while working together at the LaPorte *Herald-Argus* after I graduated from Columbia College in 1972. LaPorte, Indiana was a small factory town about seventy miles east of Chicago and it represented a chance for me to start over. At twenty-seven, after four years in the Navy and five years of college, I got my first real job.

I began my career in journalism like many a small town reporter — typing obituaries. Funeral directors delivered the information on long forms and I typed it into paragraphs. Although tedious, I learned how to deal accurately with details. My typewriter was an old black Underwood that someone on the staff said was used by Ernie Pyle. I'd read about Ernie Pyle when I was a kid and admired him. He was a war correspondent who won the Pulitzer Prize in 1944 for writing about the common soldier. His stories were written in a simple yet moving style that I tried to emulate. He was killed in battle when he was only forty-four years old.

Don Benn, editor of the *Herald-Argus*, was a small, wiry guy, about sixty-five, who wore an old-fashioned green visor. He started his career in Independence, Missouri, and covered Harry Truman back when he was a judge. Benn always prefaced names with "old."

"Yeah, old Harry was a tough judge," he'd say, "but he was fair."

Benn considered himself to be an anarchist. He said the more he saw of this world, the less he thought of government. He drank a lot and when he held a piece of copy, his hands shook.

One day, shortly after I started working at the paper, I asked him if my typewriter was really used by Ernie Pyle.

"Well," he said, scratching his neck, "Old Ernie was going to school at Indiana University when he figured he'd had enough. He got on a bus and went as far as his money could take him. He ended up in LaPorte and got himself a job on this paper. These typewriters are pretty old, and it's just possible that he could've used one of them."

That's all I needed to begin planning my future. First I would do a year on Ernie's old newspaper, then work for a bigger newspaper. Eventually I'd become a foreign correspondent dodging bullets like Ernie and reporting from exotic lands. However, for the time being, I resigned myself to living and working in a small Indiana town.

LaPorte is located in the flat farmland of Northern Indiana a few miles south of Interstate 90. It's dotted with several small lakes surrounded by houses occupied year-round and weekend cabins owned by people from Chicago. Back then Allis-Chalmers, a manufacturer of tractors and farm implements and the town's major employer, had a plant on the north edge of town. Trains supplying the plant with raw materials ran through town causing frequent traffic backups until an overpass was put in several years later. In the center of the town was a red stone courthouse surrounded by maple trees that turned fiery red, orange, and yellow in the fall. I lived in an older apartment building a couple blocks from the courthouse and enjoyed walking to work.

Mr. Moorish was the managing editor at the *Herald-Argus*. He was a slow-moving, heavy-set man nearing retirement age. He had slicked back, silvery hair and chain-smoked cigars, so a cloud of thick smoke always followed him around. Moorish was a Republican from Oregon and a staunch defender of President Richard Nixon, who was about to be impeached. He was a friendly fellow, but we had nothing in common.

One day Moorish took me to a Kiwanis banquet at the Holiday Inn where he was speaking. I had never been to a Kiwanis meeting. The banquet room was small with long tables covered in white tablecloths and arranged into a "U". Moorish introduced me to the town's business and political leaders who were seated around the table.

The meeting began with everyone singing *God Bless America*, accompanied by a frail older woman on the piano. Then someone passed out copies of the lyrics to *By the Old Mill Stream*. The letters, "P," "T," and "G" standing for "plate, table, and glass," were written above the words to the song. When the woman started playing, we all picked up a spoon and started tapping on either our plate, the table, or our glass, which produced sounds roughly in tune with the music. When the song was over, everyone laughed. I felt like a fool.

After a dinner of mashed potatoes and thin, grisly slices of roast beef in a greasy brown sauce, Moorish gave a long rambling description of the newspaper's new offset printing process. I was supposed to take notes and write a story about it, but I couldn't make much sense of his speech.

The next day I did my best to write the story, then glued the three pages end to end and took it into Moorish's office for corrections. He was seated at an old, battered, mahogany desk, smoking a cigar. He laid my story out in front of him, then leaned to the left, bracing his head with his arm. After scrutinizing my story for a long time he grabbed a pencil and began making corrections.

He wrote laboriously with heavy, jagged letters, all the while chomping tightly on his cigar as if the chomping would make the writing easier. After correcting one paragraph, he lifted the pencil, read some more, squinted through the smoke and resumed editing.

By the time he was on the third page, he was drooling on his tie and began sliding down in his chair. Having one's writing corrected was uncomfortable enough, but this was torture. After he finished, I fled to my typewriter where I tried to piece together a new article. It was no use. I told Moorish I still didn't understand the new printing process. He took pity on me and wrote the story himself. His article was as incomprehensible to me as his speech.

What saved me from the madness of the newsroom was my relationship with Dave. He turned me on to Ram Dass and was a good sounding board for my frustrations. Dave was a young man with a thin mustache who wore his dark hair in bangs across his forehead, giving him a monkish appearance. He had a Bachelor of Anthropology degree from the University of Indiana, and spoke in slow, reflective tones. Dave came from Rolling Prairie, a tiny township east of LaPorte, and was a keen observer of the local social milieu. To him, the city council meetings were "tribal gatherings" in which "esoteric utterances" were spoken. Laws were "taboos" and "mores."

That night, after my encounter with Moorish, I visited Dave at his small apartment in an old Victorian-style house with turrets that we called "The Yorkshire House" because it reminded us of a Gothic horror story.

We got high on pot and I told him about what happened.

"You should have whipped out some of this stuff and filled his cigar with it," he said, gesturing to the baggie of weed on the table.

"Yeah," I laughed. "Maybe then he would have had as much trouble understanding what he was talking about as I did." I felt myself relax and soon the petty hassles of the day seemed like nothing to get excited about.

On January 27, 1973, the Paris Peace Agreement was signed with North Vietnam, officially ending the war. By March 29, all United States ground forces had left Vietnam, American POW's were released, and the fighting was turned over to the South Vietnamese. On the national scene, evidence was uncovered linking several top White House aides with a break-in at the Democratic Party headquarters. During the summer of 1973, the Senate televised hearings on the break-in, and a special prosecutor was appointed. Impeachment hearings for President Nixon would begin in the fall.

The main editorial writer at the *Herald-Argus* was a young woman named Suzie Buckthorn. She had a BA in political science and her husband was a professor at a nearby college. Suzie had a face like a pixie with plucked eyebrows and short blonde hair. A couple months after I began working at the paper we had lunch at a local restaurant.

"You were in Vietnam, weren't you, Rich?" she asked, filing her nails while we were waiting for the food to arrive.

I usually avoided discussing politics with Suzie because she could easily outmaneuver me. However, one subject I felt secure discussing was our policy in Vietnam.

"Yeah, I spent two deployments there with the Seabees in '67 and '68," I replied. "I was in Da Nang and Chu Lai," I added, not sure if she knew where those cities were. "Up north, 'I' Corps."

Suzie began hunting for something in her purse. She looked up and said, "Oh well, I think I know where you mean. I'm glad we're letting the South Vietnamese troops take over. With all the training we've given them, they should be able to win the war."

"I'm not so sure," I said. "Without U.S. troops, I don't think they have a chance."

"I'm sure the President knows what he's doing," said Suzie. "I mean, we've spent $150 billion on the war. I'm sure it's helped a lot." She removed a gold cylinder from her purse, pulled the top off, and began applying lipstick.

I was amazed that an intelligent, educated person like Suzie could ignore the fact that there was more to winning the war than just pouring money into it.

"I don't think it's just a matter of money," I began. "You see, the North Vietnamese are fighting for something they believe in. They are fighting to reunify their country, kind of like the Civil War in the United States. I think they'll continue fighting, no matter how much money we give the South."

Suzie took out a Kleenex and blotted her lips, leaving a bright red smudge on the tissue. "What do you mean, it doesn't matter?" she said. "Of course it matters. We can bomb them into the Stone Age if we have to."

I began to feel a deep anger welling up inside. It didn't seem to matter much to her that I had been in Vietnam.

I tried again. "You've gotta understand that you could bomb the Germans and the Japanese into submission during World War II because they were highly industrialized societies. They had huge factories and rail lines that made good targets. Hell, making weapons is a cottage industry in North Vietnam. They're making guns in their homes and they're bringing them south on elephants through heavy jungles."

Suzie took a deep breath and leaned back. Just then the salad came. She speared a cucumber and nonchalantly said, "Well, at least we got a chance to test out some new weapons."

I was stunned and didn't know how to respond. Was she actually saying it was okay for 58,000 Americans to die, so we could test some new weapons? Just then the waiter brought my hamburger, a welcome diversion.

That was the last time I tried to talk with Suzie about the war. I found it increasingly difficult to work on a newspaper where the main editorial writer had such a cavalier attitude about dead soldiers.

After the first couple months on the job, the thrill of seeing my byline wore off. I had little in common with my fellow employees or the town where I worked. Instead of feeling important, I began to feel like I was stuck in the middle of nowhere. On weekends I drove to Skokie and stayed with Linda at her parent's house, sleeping on some cushions in the basement. Neither Skokie nor LaPorte offered me a sense of belonging and I began to feel alienated by both.

When Dave introduced me to Ram Dass, I began thinking less like a reporter and more like a poet. I had brief glimpses of another world where I didn't have to strive to be anything — it was enough to just be. Nevertheless, I tried to free myself from the drudgery of reporting small town news by writing about things that interested me. I wrote about a La Porte poet who worked as a bulldozer operator. I covered the Miss Nude Universe contest at a nudist camp in nearby Roselawn. However, a few interesting stories weren't enough to keep me in LaPorte. Even though I was developing a new philosophy, I was still aware that Linda and I were drifting apart. Desperate to prevent a breakup, I quit my job and moved back to Chicago where I tried to resurrect our doomed relationship.

In a couple days I would see my old friend. Maybe Dave could help me sort things out. For now though, I had to find a way out of Wells, Nevada.

30
HITCHHIKER VOODOO
Nevada Desert – August 1975

WHEN I FINISHED THE CALL to Dave, I used part of the twenty dollars Jack gave me to buy dinner. After dinner, I went back to the road and saw two other hitchhikers.

I walked up to one of them, a young, short-haired fellow, who was sitting on an Army duffel bag. "How ya doin'? "I said. "Been here long?"

"'Bout an hour."

"Well, good luck." I walked down the road and took my place in line. It was getting cold so I put on the sweater I had scrounged from the Goodwill box in Berkeley.

A few cars passed, but they were big cars. I saw them coming a mile away because the headlights were far apart. Rich people, afraid of getting ripped off. I cursed them as they blew by me like I was a weed.

"I hope you have a flat tire and freeze to death in the desert," I yelled.

After a while, the anger passed and I relaxed. I stared at the dark ridge line in the distance, silhouetted by the glow of a million stars. My mind grew calm and empty. The whoosh of cars and the chirping of crickets set up a steady mantra. I stood there until I began to shiver and the cars slowed to a trickle.

I walked back and talked to the first hitchhiker, a Marine going home on leave before shipping out for the Philippines. He seemed friendly, so I suggested we split the cost of a motel if we couldn't get a ride. He said OK. After an hour without any luck, we decided to get a room.

I helped him drag his bulky duffel bag to four motels before we finally found one we could afford. In the morning, after about five hours' sleep, we had breakfast and then flipped a coin to see who would be first in line to hitch a ride. He won. I walked east down the highway and tried to find the right spot. Sometimes a driver will pass the first hitchhiker in line and feel guilty. Seeing a second hitchhiker, he will sometimes try and redeem himself by offering a ride.

A highway sign read, DIVIDED HIGHWAY ONE MILE AHEAD. KEEP RIGHT. I stopped, turned around, and noted the speed of approaching cars. I tried to estimate when, if they passed the first guy, they would wish they hadn't, and then, how long it would take them to comfortably slow down to pick me up. I walked a little further . . . a few more steps. I looked back, studied the distance . . . four more steps. Yes, here I would make my stand.

The morning air was still cool as I looked west, the sun at my back. After about fifteen minutes, a Volkswagen appeared in the distance. VWs were always good for rides, especially the beat up, hippie ones. The bug was riding low, clutching the road. That was a good sign. He approached the soldier and passed him. Now the voodoo started working. The driver looked ahead. A lone male driver! The vibes were getting better. I wasn't sure, but he appeared to be slowing down. I casually hung my thumb out, stared into his eyes and tried to make psychic contact. For a moment the VW hung in space, then the driver pulled over and threw open the door.

I ran to his car with my pack and got in.

"Hey, man, thanks a lot. I never thought I would get out of there."

"You're quite welcome," he said, lighting up a pipe. "I'm just sorry I can't give that other guy a ride, too. I was trying to light my pipe and I just didn't see him in time."

"Well, it looks like there's plenty of traffic," I said. "He'll get out of there soon."

The sweet smell of tobacco smoke filled the car. The driver was a young professor from Stanford University driving to Boston for a teaching job.

31
OAK CREEK, COLORADO
August 1975

THE PROFESSOR TOOK ME all the way through Nevada and Utah to Oak Creek, Colorado. I planned to stay with Reilly, my buddy from Miami, for a few days. He was temporarily living in the small mountain town with a woman named Mary Claire. He met her while visiting me in Chicago when I was going to Columbia College.

I'd known Reilly since fifth grade. Back then we used to ride our bikes across the tall drawbridges, which spanned Biscayne Bay on the way to the beach. In a flat town, the bridges were the nearest things we had to mountains. The spectacular views of the blue-green water and the tall white hotels on the horizon were worth the long ride up, as was the fast, exhilarating coast down the other side.

In our senior year of high school we discovered booze. We guzzled large cans of Colt .45 Malt Liquor, then drove to the dances at the National Guard Armory in North Miami, so drunk we could barely see the road. We went to 71st Street on Miami Beach to drink beer, bake in the sun and watch the girls in tiny bikinis dance to the sounds of the jukebox at the concession stand.

Instead of going to the senior prom, we rode around Biscayne Bay at night in a friend's high-powered speedboat and got drunk on cherry flavored sloe gin mixed with beer. We passed out on Sandspur Island and spent most of the night vomiting green puke.

When we were in junior college, we worked a summer at the 1964 World's Fair as busboys and shared a room in Flushing on Long Island. We explored New York City from the Bowery and Chinatown to Greenwich Village. In New York we could drink legally at 18, but in Miami the age was 21.

When we got back home, we bought fake ID cards and continued drinking. Drinking made us feel grown up even though we both still lived at home.

It was close to sunset when the professor dropped me off in Oak Creek — population 700. The shadows of the mountains were closing in on the small town that was located at the bottom of the Yampa River valley. Railroad tracks bisected the town, and freight trains carried coal from a nearby mine.

Several years earlier, a ski resort had been planned for the area. Construction workers arrived and the town experienced a brief population boom. However, midway through the construction phase, the financing collapsed and the project was never completed. Many workers left, but others remained to collect unemployment checks and savor the Rocky Mountain lifestyle. They were mostly hippies.

After the checks stopped coming, many of them got jobs or began their own small businesses. Single women had children and collected welfare and food stamps. The hippies set up KFMU, the only wind-powered, listener-sponsored FM radio station in the country and earned the grudging respect of some of the locals. Reilly's girlfriend, Mary Claire, came to Oak Creek to help manage the resort. After the construction boom ended, she worked at the ski lift in Steamboat Springs, twenty miles to the north.

The two towns, connected by US-40, were the antithesis of each other. Oak Creek was poor and hippie, while Steamboat Springs was rich and conservative. The two-lane highway wound out of Oak Creek, down the low hills, and past the mine. At the bottom of the hills, it opened up onto a large valley with sprawling ranches. In the distance was the majestic Mt. Warner where a ski resort had been hacked out of its well-timbered flank. Steamboat Springs got its name from the hot sulfur springs located about three miles north of town at the end of a steep dirt road. The spring was owned by the county and flowed from the side of a mountain into a shallow stream. The early settlers thought the gurgling of the stream sounded like the paddles of a steamboat.

Oak Creek hippies liked to soak naked in the springs. For many, soaking in the warm waters was the only redeeming feature of Steamboat Springs. Occasionally tourists complained about nude hippies smoking dope and drinking wine at the springs. This prompted county deputies to raid the springs and arrest the hippies, reaffirming the Oak Creekers' hate and distrust of the Steamboat Springs establishment.

Although we had not spent much time together as adults, Reilly and I still shared a love of the open road. If life got too complicated, if our romantic relationships didn't work out, if the jobs became a hassle, the open highway was always there to soothe the spirit. At the end of the road, there was always Oak Creek, a refuge in the mountains populated by the spirits of the rocks and the trees and the clear, cold mountain streams.

Often we would talk about our plans for the future. When we finished talking, there would be a period of silence as our minds contemplated the infinite possibilities. Then one would say to the other, "Well, if that doesn't work out, there's always Oak Creek." We'd smile knowingly, laugh a little, and then the future wouldn't seem so foreboding. To see Reilly in Oak Creek was like coming home to a brother of the road.

Reilly had given me directions to his apartment that was located across the tracks and up a steep road. The air was turning cold and the sweet smell of sagebrush mingled with vapors of creosoted rail ties. I crossed a small bridge over the Yampa River, a small stream that rippled over round, gray pebbles. On the other side of the bridge was a rutted gravel and asphalt road. I followed the road up a steep hill to a small rectangular six-unit building on the right.

I yelled, "Crazy Reilly!" because I didn't know his apartment number. A short, slender, woman with brown hair and glasses poked her head out of a door. It was Mary Claire.

"You must be Crazy Chamberlin," she said, opening the door wide. "Crazy" was a term Reilly and I used to describe buddies from the old neighborhood in North Miami. There was "Crazy Deutsch" who became the lawyer, "Crazy Talbot" who was a helicopter pilot and died in Vietnam, and "Crazy Alpaugh" who used to get drunk and drive through the shrubs in people's yards. He became a Hollywood writer.

"How ya' doin'?" I said. "You must be Mary Claire."

"Bob!" she shouted into the other room. "Guess who's here?"

Reilly came into the living room. It took a moment for him to focus. His eyes were red from drinking beer. "Crazy Chamberlin!" he roared.

"Crazy Reilly," I roared back. We embraced.

Reilly was looking his Oak Creek finest. He had a long, untrimmed mustache and beard. His skin was weathered from the intense mountain sun and wind. His wavy blond hair was brushed back revealing a receding hairline. Reilly was shorter than I was by about four inches. As a boy, he'd been thin and wiry, but now he cultivated a beer-belly. Comparing bellies was one of our rituals. His was big and firm, but mine was thin and soft.

I looked at his belly and said, "I see you've been eating well."

"That's all muscle, Chamberlin," he replied.

He took off his shirt and tightened up his belly. "Come on Chamberlin, hit me."

Mary Claire stepped back and shook her head, "You guys!"

I delivered a punch, but Reilly just grinned

"Come on, Chamberlin, hit me harder," he roared. I stepped back and really walloped him. He just smiled.

"Okay, now it's your turn," he said, doubling up his fist. But I'd have nothing of it. I knew when I was licked. We had a good laugh.

I slept on Reilly's couch that night. The next day we decided to take an overnight hike to the Flat Tops, part of the Gore Range about a hundred miles to the northwest.

In the morning, we left Oak Creek and drove south to Phippsburg where we had breakfast at a small diner that catered to road crews. After breakfast we headed north, up a steep two-lane road. Trees began to thin out and were replaced by sagebrush. As the elevation increased they gave way to boulders covered with greenish gray lichens and dotted by patches of yellow and blue mountain flowers.

About halfway to the Flattops, a herd of sheep blocked the road. It didn't appear anyone was tending them, so I got out of the car and ran ahead, waving my hat and whooping as the sheep stampeded back onto the rocks.

About noon, we arrived at a reservoir located twelve thousand feet above sea level. I felt light-headed and began to take deep breaths, but that only made me dizzier. I started breathing from my diaphragm. That helped. The height didn't seem to bother Reilly. That pissed me off because we were always competing. When we were on the swimming team in high school he was always a little faster. He lost his virginity before me. I was especially frustrated that the draft board had found him physically unfit for military service due to a slight heart murmur, yet he continued to tour the world, sending me postcards when I was in Vietnam.

We parked the car and had some sandwiches for lunch. After we checked our gear, we began hiking up a long stone trail built through massive piles of fallen boulders. The trail climbed gradually, but soon I was gasping for air. I slowed down and Reilly started to pull ahead. He looked back.

"Come on, Chamberlin," he taunted. "Jesus, we've just started."

"You go on ahead," I panted. "Just gotta get used to this air." Talking and shouting were wasting my breath.

As we rounded the crest of the rock pile, the trail dipped along a reservoir before rising again, this time into a steep gorge. I put one foot in front of the other at a steady pace.

We hiked for another hour then rested. My feet were starting to blister so I took off my boots an cooled my feet in a shallow spring.

The wind picked up, and the temperature dropped as the sun sank lower in the sky. We hiked up the side of an ancient glacial cirque. Far below was a green plateau tinted gold by the fading sun, like a magical polo field of the gods.

By the time I reached the summit, Reilly was there waiting for me. We were on top of a narrow ridge with a vertical drop of about five hundred feet on either side. Reilly had already taken off his pack and was sitting on a rock staring at the thin strip of rocks that was our only passage forward.

"Well, Chamberlin, after you," he said, laying down the challenge.

This time I really had him. I wasn't intimidated by heights. With about two feet on either side, there was plenty of room.

"What's the matter," I crowed. "You think this is a big hairy deal? Shit. You could drive a Mack truck over this."

Reilly stared at me with a crazy look in his eyes. I walked out on the narrow rock bridge.

"Look, no hassle," I said. I walked to the edge, stood on one leg and then skipped to the other side.

Reilly's eyes darted toward me, then to the bridge. Slowly he dropped to his chest and then crawled across on his belly.

"You got me on this one, Chamberlin," he said, laughing.

The sun was just setting as we crossed the Flat Tops and began looking for some cover among the boulders and scrub juniper. Suddenly a huge buck with a magnificent rack of antlers jumped from some bushes in front of us. We were startled and then amazed as the animal quickly galloped over the ridge and disappeared on the other side. The buck had flattened the vegetation, so we decided to take its nesting area.

As soon as I dropped my pack the calves in my legs began to cramp. The muscle spasms went away when I did some stretching exercises, but then the soles of my feet began to ache. I unpacked and discovered that some of the stitching on my ten-dollar down sleeping bag was coming apart leaving thin spots. Someone once told me that to get the maximum benefit from a down bag I should sleep in the nude. I took off my clothes and climbed into the bag, but that didn't help. I wanted to put my clothes back on, but didn't want to expose my skin to the frigid air, so that night I nearly froze to death.

In the morning I had a throbbing headache. The only thing I wanted to do was get off the mountain. I quickly jumped out of the bag and threw on my clothes.

Reilly was ready to explore more country.

"Holy shit. I think my head's about to split in two," I moaned.

"I don't know about you lowlanders from Wisconsin," he said. "I guess you just can't hack it."

All right, enough of this macho posturing! My lungs required thicker air to function and my body needed energy. I removed a smashed tuna sandwich from my pack, took a couple bites and nearly threw up. I put it back and took a few swigs of water from my canteen.

We started off on a long downhill slope, but then Reilly changed direction and headed up a high, rocky grade.

"Hey, where are you goin'?" I yelled.

"I'm gonna check out the rest of this mountain," he called from a distance.

"See you at the car," I yelled.

How was I going to get down? There was no trail, only piles of broken rock and shear cliffs. My leg muscles were cramping and I was in danger of hyperventilating.

My thinking was muddled, but one thing remained very clear. I had to get down. I stopped often to catch my breath and backtracked several times after coming to the edge of a precipice.

About half-way down I heard the muffled sound of loose rocks moving. I looked up and saw a pronghorn antelope skillfully prancing over the boulders. He stopped, looked in my direction and twitched his nose. I must have seemed like a sloth or a turtle to him. Then he turned away and ran over what appeared to be a sheer cliff. Maybe the mountain gods sent him to check on me.

Slowly I picked my way down the mountain; I grew stronger as the air became richer. I located a trail and descended to a grassy area where a family of hikers was returning from an expedition. I drank some water from a mountain stream and threw up.

When I returned to the car, I stretched out on the hood and soaked up some sun. A couple hours later Reilly returned.

"Chamberlin, what happened to you?" he asked.

"Got some muscle cramps, "I said. "Just thought I'd head back and cop some rays."

"Man," he said. "You missed some beautiful views. Just over that ridge you can see all the way to Wyoming."

He was beginning to get on my nerves. "Well, I don't think I would have enjoyed it while puking my guts out," I yelled back.

He laughed. "Let's head back. There's a little diner outside of Steamboat. I'm gonna get some 'throst biff.'"

I laughed. When we had worked together at the New York World's Fair in 1964 we often ate dinner at a diner in Flushing Meadows. The waiter was Hungarian and had a thick accent. We liked to ask him what the special was just to hear him mispronounce "roast beef, peas and carrots." We'd smile at each other and try not to crack up. By the time we reached the diner in Steamboat, the nausea had passed and I joined Reilly in a roast beef dinner.

"Hey, Chamberlin," he said after we finished. Why don't we wash down the dinner with a little apéritif."

"Like what," I asked.

"I was thinking of a little sloe gin."

"I don't think so," I laughed. "I'd like to keep this food down."

On the way back to Oak Creek we stopped at the hot springs. It was getting dark and a full moon was rising. The scalding hot water, which flowed from the side of the hill into the stream, had been diverted into pools and each pool was a different temperature. We shimmied down the steep bank and stripped, leaving our clothes on the rocks. As I waded across the churning stream to reach the pools, the pebbles tickled my feet and the icy waters took my breath away.

"Reilly, this is freezin'," I yelled.

"Come on, Chamberlin. What are you, a pussy?"

Reilly was right behind me, and as I stood there trying to get my balance, he whipped past me. When I reached the pools I began testing their water temperature with my toe. I found a pool that was lukewarm and gradually lowered myself into it. The sweetness of the spruce trees, the rotten egg odor of sulfur springs and the pungent smoke of nearby campfires combined to produce a heavenly aroma. The tops of the trees were bathed in the white light of the moon, and the gurgling of the stream slowly put me into a trance. The painful memory of the hike soon dissipated like the steam rising up from the springs. After a while I got used to the warm water, so I moved to a hotter pool. While I was floating there, a middle-aged couple slipped into a nearby pool and invited us to share some wine. About an hour later we left, mellowed out and ready for a good night's rest.

There was just one more mountain range to go until I got to Dave's.

32
HORSE HEAVEN
Fort Collins, Colorado – August 1975

I LEFT OAK CREEK in the morning and headed for Fort Collins where Dave Crum was attending Colorado State University. I hitched north to Steamboat Springs, then east on US-40. The road climbed steeply and was equipped with runaway truck ramps, long flat strips covered with thick gravel. On top of the pass was a stretch of broken boulders with a rock formation that looked like two rabbit ears. From Granby I got a ride on US-34 to Rocky Mountain National Park.

Later that afternoon I was let off on a high plain just inside the western gate. Traffic was sparse except for the occasional dark sedan filled with senior citizens. As they drove by, they peered at me through rolled up windows like I was part of the wildlife. Signs warned *No Overnight Camping* and *No Hitchhiking*, my two main modes of survival.

I couldn't get a ride, so after sunset I camped on top of a granite rock outcropping about one hundred yards from the main highway. I was about to fall asleep when I heard the low drone of an engine coming up the road. I looked up and saw a flash of light. I scrambled for my glasses as a searchlight swept toward me, across an open field. It was probably a ranger looking for illegal campers. I jumped out of my bag and dropped into a nearby crevice, dragging the bag with me. Seconds later the beam passed over my spot. The truck continued down the road, past my position and out of sight. I climbed back on top of the rocks and tried to get some sleep, but I was too angry. Someone might have reported me. What was I doing to hurt anyone? I was just trying to get some sleep.

The next morning I waited by the road until tourists started trickling in and eventually got a ride to Estes Park. With its garish assortment of tourist shops, Estes Park was, to me, the antithesis of the Rocky Mountains. Yet, the irony was that the rugged, individualistic mountain men, the first white men to set their eyes on the beauty of this incredible wilderness, were the forerunners of industrial tourism. Instead of selling tee-shirts to tourists, they sold fur to Europeans. When the beavers were trapped out and the fashions changed, they were out of business.

As the road descended east of the park, I discovered that my ears were plugged. I tried to clear them by yawning, but couldn't. By the time I reached the foothills, I was half deaf.

When I got to the outskirts of Fort Collins I called Dave from a taco stand, then sat at a table on the patio and waited for him to pick me up. The jagged outline of the mountains was visible on the western horizon, but disappeared into the gray haze of Denver to the south

I was just finishing up my Coke at Taco Bell, trying to yawn and clear my plugged-up ears, when Dave drove up in a beat-up white Toyota. He got out of the car and I walked halfway to meet him. He was a quiet, private guy so we just clenched each other's shoulders in a kind of half-hug.

"How ya doin'?" I asked.

"Fine. And yourself?"

"Great. Just trying to get my ears to pop. I think I got some water in them yesterday at the hot springs." I threw my head to the side and slapped the area above my temple with the palm of my hand.

"God, you look wild," he said, staring at me.

"Yeah, well, this life on the road will do that to you." I felt a little uneasy about being stared at. "So what have you been doing this summer?"

"Oh, I've been working part-time at the graduate library and doing some day hikes in the area," he said.

Dave was living with his girlfriend from LaPorte. She was a quiet young woman with dark brown bangs that descended past her eyebrows. "How's Linda," I asked. "She workin'?"

"She's fine," said Dave. "She works as a cashier at a grocery store near the apartment."

I threw my pack into the back seat and we headed to his apartment on the outskirts of town.

"In your letter you said you were applying to grad school for anthro," I said. "Have you been accepted?"

"Not yet, but they liked my application. I wrote a sociological study of the Indiana State Prison."

"I'm sure they did," I said. Dave had the knack of looking at life through the eyes of the social scientist, yet his objectivity was tempered with compassion for others. Once I'd asked him what his solution was to rehabilitating hardened criminals. He said he would hire only guards who knew how to love.

I wanted to talk with Dave about the world of spirit, the world he had introduced me to with Ram Dass's book when we worked together at the LaPorte *Herald-Argus*. I wanted to share my insights about reality with him, but the time never seemed right.

Dave, Linda and I took some bike rides, saw a movie and drove around the mountains. But the longer we spent together, the more it seemed inappropriate for me to start a conversation about Ram Dass. Although I had taken his teachings to heart, it seemed like they were now part of Dave's past.

I had to break the ice somehow. That night Dave and I were sitting on his second-story porch, having a beer at sunset. What the hell, I thought. Now is as good a time as any.

"I've been meaning to ask you about something," I said.

"What's that?'

"Ram Dass."

"What about Ram Dass?"

"Well," I started out. I stopped. It was hard to put into words. "It's the ego thing. I've been trying to let go of my ego . . . trying to see through this shoddy veil we call reality."

Dave smiled a little and shook his head. "I remember you telling me about the first time you did acid and lost your ego. It sounded like a bad experience, right?"

"Yeah, I thought I was losing my mind,"

"You were, but you got it back."

"Yeah."

"How did you feel when you got it back?"

"I felt good," I said. I took a swig of beer.

"So, it's good to have an ego," said Dave.

"Well, yeah. I guess you need it," I said wondering where this was leading.

"Don't leave home without it," said Dave. We laughed. "So how come you did it again?"

"Well, I thought it would be better the second time," I said. "Like, I would know better how to control it. At least this time I didn't lose my ego."

"Congratulations," said Dave, with a tone of sarcasm in his voice. "You came out with the same thing you went in with."

"I hope you don't mind me saying this," Dave said slowly, his words measured, "but I think you're using Ram Dass like you used drugs — to avoid reality."

"Not exactly," I said. "Acid showed me that what we think of as reality is really just a commonly held belief system and each culture builds a slightly different version of this system to fit its needs."

"You've got my attention," said Dave. "Go on."

I took another swig of my beer. "If someone's thinking goes too far out of bounds out of the system they are often labeled insane. Acid takes you out of the system. Today we're living in a system where science and logic have given us a pretty good lifestyle. We stopped burning witches long ago and have already been to the moon. . . ."

"So what does all this have to do with acid?" asked Dave. "I'm not following you."

"Don't you see? With all our scientific understanding most people still believe in God. We can't empirically prove the existence of God because our God is somehow outside our system, yet those who believe in a deity are not labeled insane. Not at all — in fact we've built up an elaborate hierarchy of churches and theology to support this belief. Do we possess a double standard when it comes to reality? It appears we do. This is where God and LSD meet. At that point of contact there is a little hole that I slipped through that allowed me to explore."

"Like the rabbit hole in *Alice in Wonderland*," said Dave. "Go on, Alice."

I stood up and curtseyed. "This is the connection that's shared by the true mystics of all religions. I wasn't raised Christian and felt uncomfortable with what I saw of it growing up, but for some reason I became fascinated by the nature of reality."

"How were you raised?" asked Dave. "I remember you saying something once about your father and a Bible case."

"Yeah," I said. "He sued the public schools in Florida for Bible reading and won. He was an atheist and I think he saw the suit as the major accomplishment of his life, yet. . . ." I stared out at the field. The sun was getting lower as a broad band of clouds moved in from the south. Suddenly the image of my father flashed in my head. We were taking a walk together.

I heard a voice. "Hello . . . earth to Richard. You were saying?"

"Oh yeah. Sorry. I remember taking a walk with my dad before he died. About four years ago my parents were living at an apartment complex in Louisville, Kentucky. They had moved back there from South Carolina where my father suffered a near-fatal heart attack about six months earlier. I was on spring break from Columbia College. One day my dad and I took a walk. The weather was cold and cloudy and we were both bundled up. My dad wore a beige trench coat and a black hat with the brim pulled tightly over his head. He looked so small and fragile; I wanted to put my arms around him to protect him from the cold . . . from the darkness . . . from death . . . but I knew that would have made him feel uncomfortable."

I took a deep breath and slowly exhaled.

"Anyway, we began our walk in the parking lot. One treeless road led from the lot to a couple of gas stations near the interstate highway. My mother had told us not to walk too far, only a half-mile round trip, doctor's orders. As we left the lot, a few cars passed us and we moved closer to the edge of the road. I asked him how he was doing."

"'Oh, hells bells, I'm doing well enough, I guess,' he answered."

"'You know, you're lucky to be alive,' I said." 'We didn't think you were going to make it. You've been given another chance at life.'"

"My father was unusually quiet and I could tell he was turning something over in his mind. About half-way to the gas station he stopped and gazed into the distance. He sighed, raised his shoulders into a shrug and extended his palms."

"'What does it all mean?'"

"I put my head down and ran my fingers through my hair. He turned to face me. My father was asking me for the meaning of life. Wasn't it supposed to be the other way around? I looked up and then turned away. I felt helpless."

"'I don't know,' I answered."

I brought the beer bottle to my mouth and stared at the clouds. Dave didn't say anything.

"You know, I've thought about that moment for a long time," I went on. "My father knew he was coming to the end of the road, but with his scientific mind he was never able to deduct any general field theory for the meaning of life. Since he was unable to find one for himself, he never tried to impose one on me. He probably didn't know it, but my father gave me a precious gift, the freedom to find my own meaning in life."

"So what is the meaning of life?" asked Dave.

"Go get me another beer and I'll tell ya," I said.

Dave went to the refrigerator and came back with a cold beer. I popped the top with an opener, took a long drink and burped.

"Is that the meaning of life?" said Dave. "I knew it had to be something simple yet profound."

The wind was blowing harder and a small cyclone twisted its way across the prairie kicking up dust.

"No. I'm getting to it, just give me some time. When I got back from Vietnam I was really pissed off at the government. Four years of my life had been wasted. The Viet Cong won and 58,000 American soldiers died — for what? Vietnam showed me the hypocrisy of this society. I felt complicit with that society. I needed to cleanse myself. Acid took me out of that society . . . no . . . wait . . . acid took the society out of me."

Dave's eyes got big and he gave me a crazed look. "Are we getting a flashback here?"

I laughed. "Well, I'm done with that stuff now. Anyway, this was still my country and I had to try to live in it. I wanted to fit in, yet when I tried, I felt like an impostor. I felt empty inside and began looking for something to fill the void. I thought love was the answer."

"Ah yes, love," said Dave. "I can see it in the eyes of the Hare Krishnas, truly something beautiful to behold."

"No, it wasn't anything like that. You remember Linda, don't you?"

"How could I forget?" said Dave. "You used to talk with me for hours about your hassles with her."

"My spiritual quest really began with her."

"Yeah, I remember," said Dave. "She didn't think you were spiritual enough." He got up and went to the cupboard. "You want some tortilla chips?"

I could tell Dave didn't want to talk about it, but I needed to put the relationship in context for him.

He came back and placed bowls of chips and salsa on the table.

"OK," he said, checking his watch.

"When I met Linda, she felt desperately alone and I loved comforting her. After she began to feel better, she threw herself into painting and music and wanted to share this passion with me, but we never connected that way. She accused me of being insensitive and challenged me to find my own passion to share."

"Yeah, I remember. She wanted Clark Kent reporter to become Superman," teased Dave.

"Don't interrupt; this won't take long," I said. "Soon the hassle over the quote *passion issue* unquote drained my ability to feel anything and caused me to resent her. When we couldn't work things out, she cut me loose."

Dave checked his watch. "I'm still waiting for the meaning of life here."

"It's coming, don't worry," I said. "Linda actually did me a huge favor. She set me adrift believing that I was spiritually deficient. That motivated me to confront my life, why am I here and how do I find true love."

"And don't forget, 'How do I get laid?' too."

We laughed and shared the chips and salsa. A chilly wind whipped down from the mountains.

"So what about Ram Dass?" said Dave. "What do you think about the 'acid guru' these days?"

"Well, say what you will about him, but after I went to see him in Madison, things began to come together and make sense. He embodied the spirituality I never got from my father, so in that respect he was the father I never had. He gave me a context that explained what happened when I took LSD. I learned that the world is what you perceive it to be. Did you ever hear him talk about the big ice cream cone in the sky?"

"No, but I think I'm gonna hear it now," said Dave.

"Yes, you are. Well, everybody wants the big ice cream cone in the sky and you've got to eat if before it melts. Then when it's gone, you've got this taste in your mouth, so you've gotta have a glass of water to get rid of the taste. Then you've got this bloated feeling in your stomach and you try and walk it off. It gets cold outside and you decide to get some hot chocolate to warm up; the process of satisfying your senses goes on and on. It's called life. The secret to living isn't getting everything you need because you can never get enough. Suffering is not the lack of stuff. Suffering is caused by the constant need for stuff. And we can never get enough stuff, so we will never be satisfied."

"That sounds familiar."

"Once you realize this, you struggle with it until you reach peace of mind," I said. "Some people struggle with it the rest of their lives; they just decide to suffer. It all depends on your karma."

"And have you got enough stuff?" asked Dave.

"I don't know," I said. "I'm still struggling. Stuff comes in many forms. I'm not starving and I'm not sick and I've got a place to sleep tonight. Yet, sometimes I want to see into the other dimensions. There are probably other parallel worlds out there . . . no . . . right here in front of us."

Dave rested his eyes on the pasture next to the apartment building. I squinted into the setting sun. Below us in the field, two gray quarter horses stomped and snorted as they played in the corral. Their nostrils flared, emitting bursts of white steam into the chilly evening air. Rays of golden sunshine fanned out from behind purple clouds and cast a reddish-yellow hue on the scene below us. The sweet aroma of blooming sagebrush and wet earth drifted on the breeze. I squinted and tried to see through the scene to a parallel universe even more wondrous.

Dave took a swig of beer and just stared off into the distance. Then, in a slightly aggravated tone he said, "How could anything be more beautiful and mind-blowing than this, watching these beautiful creatures run around as the sky is lit on fire?"

I opened my mouth to reply, but nothing came out. The sun had set, the evening was coming on and with Dave, I listened as the cicadas began chirping in the trees.

EPILOGUE
Columbia, South Carolina
Spring 1981

IN THE SPRING OF MY thirty-sixth year I had no idea what I was going to do with my life. My last big scheme, to become a real estate investor with my mother in Columbia, South Carolina, turned into a disaster. Real estate wasn't moving in 1981; interest rates were too high.

After living on my own for sixteen years, I was reduced to living with my mother in a rented townhouse, without a job or even a plan for the future. I had bottomed out. In desperation I began to ask myself, where did I go wrong or, more importantly, what was there inside of me, an educated middle-class white boy, that had brought me to this point? I was trying to put the pieces together.

But thinking about my predicament just made it worse. There were times when I would just turn off my brain and imagine that I was an imbecile. That worked until I had to make a decision. What kind of job did I want to apply for? Where did I want to live? Who was I? Sometimes I'd become short of breath and feel like I was about to have a heart attack. I'd lie down, try to breathe slowly, and tell myself it was all in my imagination.

Late one afternoon I was driving home from the grocery store. The trees along the two-lane road leading to our apartment were beginning to show signs of green. Here and there a dogwood tree was putting out pink and white blossoms, which were in danger of being choked by the voracious kudzu vines that blanketed the forest. Suddenly I was seized by an overwhelming moment of sadness and desperation. I was so tired of thinking, tired of living. Death seemed like a comforting friend. I searched the shoulder of the road for a strong, tall telephone pole, one that could withstand an impact without breaking. I figured that if I hit it squarely enough I could die in an instant. But I would have to do the job right. My hands began to shake and the steering wheel slid beneath my sweating palms.

I began to cry and the tears made a blur of the road in front of me. It would be so easy. A second of pain and it would be all over. I locked my arms out straight and managed to hold the car on the road. In a moment the urge passed and I regained control.

When I got home I was shaken and told my mother what happened. She had been trying to help me, but I needed something she couldn't provide. She suggested that I visit the VA hospital and get into a Vietnam veteran's support group. As much as I hated to admit it, I was in serious need of some therapy.

The next day I went to the hospital and asked a young woman at the information booth in the lobby who I could see about getting some counseling.

"You'd better go to the outpatient desk at the other end of the building," she said pointing down a long hall.

The word "patient" stuck in my brain. I didn't think of myself as a patient. I just wanted to talk with someone.

"Thanks," I said and began walking down the hall.

On the way I noticed a sign on an office saying SOCIAL WORKER. I walked in. A black, middle-aged woman with a plaque on her desk indicating she had Masters of Social Work (MSW) was going through some papers.

"Hi," I said cautiously. "Sorry for interrupting."

She looked up.

"I was just wondering if I can talk with someone in a Vietnam veteran's outreach program."

"I think they were going to get something started up in Greenville but they never did." She held up her finger and said, "Just a minute and let me check on that for you."

After making a couple of phone calls she said, "We can get you in a program, but they'll have to get you admitted at the outpatient desk. Just go down the hall and see the girl at the desk and she'll walk you through."

I disliked the idea of being "admitted" even more than being branded a "patient" I began to feel dizzy and leaned against the wall.

Perhaps she sensed my desperation, because before I left, she jotted the letters "DAV" (Disabled American Veterans) and a phone number on a piece of paper.

"You might want to look into this," she said handing it to me.

I left her office in a half-daze and wandered down the hall to the outpatient desk where I told another young woman that I had been referred by the social worker.

"Let me see your papers," she asked briskly.

My mind went blank. My papers . . . my papers . . . oh, they probably wanted my DD-214, my discharge papers. "Oh, you mean my DD-214?" I asked. "They're at home somewhere."

She gave me an incredulous look and said, "You mean you don't have a file?"

"This is my first time here," I said.

"Well, first you've got to see a doctor," she said. "It's standard procedure." She said the words, "standard procedure" as if an iron door had just clanged shut. She placed a form in front of her, picked up a pen and asked, "Now, what is your name?"

"I don't want to see a doctor."

She picked up a telephone and dialed turning away from me. I caught snatches of her conversation.

"No, he doesn't want to see a doctor . . . I don't know . . . seems a little nervous."

Finally I couldn't stand waiting anymore and left.

Eventually I got into a Vietnam veteran's support group sponsored by the DAV. The meetings took place after hours in the basement of a church in downtown Columbia. They were facilitated by Dr. Culver, a vet himself. He was a tall man in his thirties, slightly overweight, and used a cane to walk.

There were six of us at the first meeting and we sat in a semicircle in front of Dr. Culver. "Welcome to the group," he said, in a slow southern drawl. "In the daytime I have a private practice, but now I'm off the clock, so I don't want to get into a lot of psychoanalyzing bullshit."

I liked him already.

"I've got three rules," said Dr. Culver. "One. Whatever happens here stays here. Two. You don't insult each other. And three, you don't blame anything on the war."

"Shit man," said a guy with slicked back hair. "Whattaya mean you can't blame anything on the war. Isn't that why we're all here?"

Everyone shifted around in their seats, smiled a little nervously, and looked at Dr. Culver.

"The war's over," he said. "Blaming the war isn't going to help you deal with anything. It's just a convenient excuse. We're going to learn to try and solve problems in the here and now."

It was silent.

Dr. Culver lifted a cup of coffee from the floor and took a drink. "Why don't we go around the circle and you can each tell us a little bit about yourself — or not, whatever you feel comfortable with. I'll start out. I was a First Lieutenant in the Army and stepped on a mine near Pleiku in 1969. I almost lost both my legs," he said, tapping the cup on his thigh. It sounded hollow. "After my discharge I bounced around from job to job, indulged in a few too many drugs, and ended up getting help from the VA. I decided to go back to school and become a psychologist."

There was a pause as he looked around the circle. "Who wants to go next?"

The guy with the slicked back hair was the first one to volunteer. He was well-muscled and had a pale complexion. "My name is Leonard," he said. "I'm a truck driver." Leonard crossed his arms and stared at the floor.

A slim man wearing a suit spoke next. "I'm Thomas. I'm not really sure why I'm here. I heard this group was forming and I just thought I'd see what was going on." He had a quiet voice and a slight lisp.

It was silent for a while and Dr. Culver took another sip of coffee.

"My name is Richard," I said. "I can't seem to get my life together. I feel like I should be married and have a good job, but nothing's working out." I didn't mention that two weeks earlier I had nearly tried to kill myself by driving my car into a tree.

"Shit, man," said Leonard. "I wish I wasn't married. My ol' lady's driving me crazy. I got three kids and all I can think of is when I was in 'Nam. I'd be driving down the road with my 60-millimeter locked and loaded and I was a bad motherfucker. I was somebody. No one messed with me."

A black man with a goatee and wire-rimmed glasses looked up and smiled, but didn't say anything.

A vet with a ponytail who had been staring vacantly at the corner of the room was next. He put his hands behind his head and looked around. "I guess I'm the only motherfucker left," he said. "I'm here because my parole officer thought it was a good idea." He lit a cigarette. "Fucker said I had an anger management problem."

We went around and talked a little more about how fucked up everything was and I began to feel less alone.

I went to a couple more sessions and began feeling better. I don't know exactly why, but maybe it just helped to see that there were other veterans who were having trouble adjusting, too. Maybe I stopped blaming things on the war.

My mother encouraged me to write as a form of therapy. I didn't know what to write about, so I began writing about my life. Eventually I moved back to Madison and continued writing. When I was finished, I put my writing away for a while. From time to time I'd take it out, shape and revise it, then set it aside again. Eventually it began to morph into a hitchhiking story. At first I was using the working title, *Hitchhiker*, but someone at a writer's conference suggested *Hitchhiking From Vietnam*.

☯

Several years ago, before he had a stroke, Ram Dass came to Madison to speak. By chance, I ran into him near the baggage carousel at the airport.

I walked up to him and said, "Welcome to Madison."

He looked up and smiled.

"You know, I've been a follower of yours for a long time," I said.

"I've been a follower of yours, too," he answered, not missing a beat.

We both laughed.

THE END

ABOUT THE AUTHOR

Richard Chamberlin has a BA in Journalism from Columbia College and has been a newspaper reporter, freelance writer, psychiatric nurse and cab driver. He lives in the small town of Monona just outside of Madison, Wisconsin with his wife.

Printed in the United States
74277LV00001B/25-111